Presented To:

From:

Date:

The 23rd Psalm

The 23rd Psalm

Enjoying God's Best in the Midst of a Storm

Mitchell H. Warren

DESTINY IMAGE® PUBLISHERS, INC.
P.O. Box 310,
Shippensburg, PA 17257-0310

"Promoting Inspired Lives"

This book and all other Destiny Image, Revival Press, MercyPlace, Fresh Bread, Destiny Image Fiction, and Treasure House books are available at Christian bookstores and distributors worldwide.

For a U.S. bookstore nearest you, call 1-800-722-6774.
For more information on foreign distributors, call 717-532-3040.
Reach us on the Internet: www.destinyimage.com.

ISBN 13 TP: 978-0-7684-3955-7
ISBN 13 Ebook: 978-0-7684-8939-2

For Worldwide Distribution, Printed in the U.S.A.
3 4 5 6 7 8 9 10 11 / 13 12

Acknowledgments

I would like to thank my first mentor, Pastor R.G. Hardy, who faithfully taught me the principles of the faith in my early years of ministry and instilled in me a love for the Word of God. I thank Apostle Aaron B. Claxton for showing me through word and deed how a true man of God should fulfill his calling and do the work of the ministry.

Many thanks to all the members of the Word and Faith Fellowship family for their support and prayers. Thanks to my mom, spiritual advisor, confidante, and friend, Minister Marlene Epps, for her godly advice and prayers.

Thanks to my children, Mitchell, Michelle, and Joshua for the blessing you have been in my life and for serving as inspiration for many of the lessons I've learned and shared in this book. And to Darlene, my wife, for your continual love and support and for your work in editing the original manuscript.

Above all, humble thanks to God, my Good Shepherd, for giving me the inspiration, persistence, and wisdom to finish this project. To You be all the glory, honor, and praise.

Contents

Prologue

Psalm 23 is appropriately placed between two other prophetic passages, Psalms 22 and 24. Taken together, these three texts foretell the life and ministry as well as the death and subsequent resurrection of Jesus Christ. Psalm 22 reveals Christ in His *past* ministry as *Prophet* and suffering Servant of God. Psalm 24 reveals Christ in His *future* ministry as the reigning *King* triumphantly returning to the earth. Psalm 23 reveals Christ in His *present*-day ministry as *Priest* and Good Shepherd over the flock of God, the Church. Jesus' ministry, as it relates to God's eternal plan of redemption for man, can be understood by examining these three offices of prophet, priest, and king.

The Church has taught, explained, and sung about the life and ministry of Jesus, including His death, burial, and resurrection, and correctly so. Without Calvary and the resurrection there would be no Church. The Church has also taught and sung about the second coming of Christ to the earth. And certainly, we should always anticipate and look for the imminent return of Christ to the earth for His Church. However, it is equally important that each believer understands Christ's present-day ministry to the Church. We are currently living in a time when personal faith and basic biblical principles are being challenged in every part of our society. The apostle Paul described these times:

> *This know also, that in the last days perilous times shall come. For men shall be lovers of their own selves, covetous, boasters, proud, blasphemers, disobedient to parents, unthankful, unholy, without natural affection, trucebreakers, false accusers, incontinent, fierce, despisers of those that are good, traitors, heady, highminded, lovers of pleasures more than lovers of God* (2 Timothy 3:1-4).

More than ever, you need the nourishment, guidance, and protection of the Good Shepherd for you and your family. The Lord will stand by you no matter what the circumstances. The Good Shepherd will *never* flee when danger or difficulties arise. We have witnessed the failure of man's political, social, and economic systems when they refuse to acknowledge God as their source. Do not put your trust in Wall Street, Main Street, or the White House. Put your trust in the

Good Shepherd who will lead you to success and the fulfillment of your creative purpose in this life.

Introduction

I can remember when I was a little boy hearing the old folks talk about the good old days. They would talk about the times when their neighborhoods where so safe that you could go anywhere in the community at any time of the day or night and still feel safe. You could leave your kids with neighbors and trust that they would be taken care of. There were no concerns of them being harmed when you dropped them off at school. There were no drug dealers lurking in the dark waiting for an opportunity to peddle their poison. And there were no predators on the Internet attempting to lure our children into a dangerous and sometimes deadly trap using false promises of fun and excitement. When difficult times or personal tragedies did come, you were able to rely on family, neighbors, and the church. Even the government was a source of relief and assistance to those who may not have had their own support system in place.

Boy, have things changed! More and more families have become dysfunctional and fragmented. In fact, the structure of a nuclear family—a husband, a wife, and the children—only exist in about half of all homes in America.[1] People now live in neighborhoods for ten years and still do not know who their neighbors are. Churches were once the center of the local community. The church was a gathering place for families and friends. You could go there and get healing for your body, comfort for your soul, peace for your mind, forgiveness for your heart, counsel for your family, and guidance for daily living. Unfortunately, many churches have become little more than social gathering places where very little spiritual healing takes place.

And what about the government? Are you kidding? Remember when the government was a source of help to the poor and less fortunate in our society? Politicians didn't promise to solve all your problems, but did strive to uphold their constitutional duties to establish justice, ensure domestic tranquility, provide for the common defense, promote the general welfare, and secure the blessings of liberty to ourselves and our posterity.[2] Now, we seem to be paying for a whole lot more government, but receiving a whole lot less in return.

As you read the daily news or watch any of the myriad of network and cable news broadcasts, you will notice that we are constantly bombarded with one tragic story after another. As soon as one problem is resolved another two greater issues take center stage. There are crises in our families. We have broken homes producing broken kids who in turn produce more broken kids, and the cycle starts all over again. There are crises in our cities. There is rising unemployment, rising crime rates, rising teen pregnancies, and ever-increasing cases of sexually transmitted diseases. Even small, rural communities have their share of troubles. Many of our schools are experiencing financial and academic distress. Financial markets have collapsed worldwide. The environment is said to be deteriorating at an accelerated rate. Government leaders appear to be in complete disarray as they scramble to find solutions that they hope will work. The leaders make grandiose promises that they unfortunately cannot deliver. In fact, our political leaders spend more time fighting with each other than they do solving the problems they were elected to deal with. Many religious institutions and their leaders have lost their effectiveness to address these problems due to a number of high profile revelations of misconduct and abuse.

In addition to all this, there are wars and threats of war springing up around the globe. International crises exist on every continent. Domestic and foreign terrorism threaten our national security. These conditions that we are seeing today were predicted by Jesus two millennia ago.

> *And ye shall hear of wars and rumours of wars: see that ye be not troubled: for all these things must come to pass, but the end is not yet. For nation shall rise against nation, and kingdom*

against kingdom: and there shall be famines, and pestilences, and earthquakes, in divers places. All these are the beginning of sorrows (Matthew 24:6-8).

As a result, this generation, in spite of the wonderful advances in science, medicine, and technology, has become more cynical, sick, depressed, and violent. The pharmaceutical companies have become multi-billion dollar enterprises. Hospitals and medical centers are booming with business. The psychiatric profession is strained to capacity with an ever-increasing case load. Cheap substitutes such as alcohol, various legal and illegal drugs, hedonism, and mindless entertainment have done little to satisfy our need for peace of mind, provide a sense of direction, or lead to fulfillment in life. The effect of these conditions was also predicted by Jesus.

Men's hearts failing them for fear, and for looking after those things which are coming on the earth: for the powers of heaven shall be shaken (Luke 21:26).

Notice Jesus said men's hearts would fail just from *looking* at the things that are happening in the news. It should not surprise us that heart disease is the number one killer in our society.[3] I will admit that on the surface this is a pretty bleak picture with no apparent solution in sight. Fortunately, this is only half of the picture. The good news is that God has provided, through His Word, the wisdom, guidance, and the power necessary for us to rise above the confusion of this life. God wants you to experience His *peace, power, provision,* and *protection* today.

For the past 25 years I have had the blessed privilege of pastoring a thriving urban church ministry. As pastor I have had the opportunity to counsel hundreds of individuals and families. Many of these wonderful families were experiencing difficult situations such as a financial crisis or the loss of a loved one. I thank God that I was able to offer godly wisdom and comfort to them during such a trying time in their lives. At times like these, I have often heard ministers and Christians use Psalm 23 to bring comfort and consolation to those who are hurting. This beautiful passage certainly does bring a sense of peace to many during a time of sorrow and loss.

However, I want to show you through the Word of God that Psalm 23 has little to do with the hereafter, but everything to do with our present, everyday lives. God has revealed powerful truths in each verse of Psalm 23. Every word is power-packed with a twofold purpose and meaning. First, each verse contains valuable insight into the daily lives of typical Bedouin shepherds as they have plied their trade for thousands of years. Second, each verse contains golden nuggets of truth that reveal God's awesome provisions for our care and protection. These provisions are ours to enjoy daily because of the present-day ministry of Jesus Christ, our Good Shepherd.

Recently, I took my family to Ocean City, Maryland, for a summer vacation. The weather was ideal for this time of year with blue, sunny skies during the day and clear, cool nights. We especially enjoyed sitting on the beach in our lounge chairs, taking in the sun and listening to the waves as they crashed into the sand. Later that year during the winter time, my wife and I decided to go back to the beach for a little rest and relaxation. After checking into our room, we ventured out of the room and headed to the beach. At a particular opening leading to the beach, we noticed this sign hanging across the pathway on a chain: "Closed for the Season." We were obviously disappointed as we headed back to our room. The sign made me think about what so many of you are experiencing in your lives today. For too many, the *season of blessing* has been *closed* for a long time. So have the seasons of *healing*, *prosperity*, and *peace*. It is time for the new season to open! This is *your season* for a *breakthrough!*

As you prayerfully read this book, let the fresh *Rhema* (God's living Word) penetrate your heart and mind. Read it all the way through and go back and read it again. I am absolutely convinced that the truths revealed in these pages *will change your life!*

Finally, it is my prayer that, first, the Holy Spirit will give to you a spirit of wisdom and understanding into this present-day ministry of Jesus Christ your Good Shepherd, and second, you will use this knowledge to rise above the circumstances of your life and begin to experience the fullness of God's blessings for you.

Endnotes

1. Family Structure and Children's Health in the United States; Findings from The National Health Interview Survey, 2001-2007 Center for Disease Control and Prevention/National Center for Health Statistics accessed 3/11/2011, http://www.cdc.gov/nchs/sr_10/sr10_246.pdf.

2. The Constitution of the United States of America, preamble, http://topics.law.cornell.edu/constitution/preamble.

3. FastStats, "Leading Causes of Death," Centers for Disease Control and Prevention, December 31, 2009, Number of deaths for leading causes of death, accessed February 18, 2011, http://www.cdc.gov/nchs/fastats/lcod.htm.

CHAPTER 1

The Lord Is My Shepherd

(JEHOVAH-ROHI)
THE LORD WHO IS MY SHEPHERD

Psalm 23 is one of the most inspiring chapters in the Bible. Its words give us comfort and hope during times of trouble. Songs have been sung using the words of this beautiful passage to uplift the hearts of millions of people during times of bereavement and loss. What we will see, however, is that God had infinitely more in mind when He inspired David to pen these verses.

The first picture we see of David in the Bible is that of a young teenager watching over his father's sheep on the backside of a mountain (see 1 Sam. 16:11). It was at this time that David received his calling from the Lord and was anointed by the prophet Samuel. While tending to his father's sheep, David encountered many challenges that threatened the safety of his father's flock. Wild beasts presented one of the greatest threats to the sheep.

The shepherd had to be prepared to protect the flock with his own life if necessary. This was true even if the sheep did not personally belong to the shepherd. In addition, the shepherd was responsible for feeding the sheep. This required the constant search for suitable pastures for grazing and finding drinkable water to nourish the flock.

The shepherd's job was often a very lonely occupation as well as a potentially dangerous one. On one of these lonely nights, not unlike many others that preceded it, I imagine David, during a quiet moment, looked up into the starry sky and began to understand his role as shepherd of his father's sheep. He realizes that he cares for his father's sheep in the same way God cares for him. This prompted David to pen these powerful words:

> *The Lord is my shepherd; I shall not want. He maketh me to lie down in green pastures: He leadeth me besides the still waters. He restoreth my soul: He leadeth me in the paths of righteousness for His name's sake. Yea, though I walk through the valley of the shadow of death, I will fear no evil: for Thou art with me; Thy rod and Thy staff they comfort me. Thou preparest a table before me in the presence of mine enemies: Thou anointest my head with oil; my cup runneth over. Surely goodness and mercy shall follow me all the days of my life: and I will dwell in the house of the Lord for ever* (Psalm 23).

David recognizes that God is his shepherd and that He has been providing for him all his life. As David thinks about how good God has been to him, he recounts the many times that wild beasts have come against the sheep to devour them. David also thinks about the times there was no water to nourish the flock or grass feed them. David understood that as a shepherd the sheep were completely dependent on him. He alone bore the sole responsibility for protecting and providing for the sheep. As David meditates on these things, he no doubt realizes that *God Himself* is just as responsible for protecting and providing for him as he is for the sheep. What David understands is that God's Fatherly care was *not* something he expected to enjoy sometime in the future, but it was what God provided for him right now, today. David spoke from experience when he declared:

> *I have been young, and now am old; yet have I not seen the righteous forsaken, nor his seed* [children] *begging bread* (Psalm 37:25).

One minister years ago said it this way: "The Lord is my shepherd; He's all I need." Take a moment to meditate on the magnitude of this statement. *Selah* (a musical term which means to pause for a moment). Do you remember the old saying, "It's not what you know but who you know that counts"? That statement most assuredly applies when it comes to our Good Shepherd! What kind of shepherd do *you* have? What are His qualifications? Is He able to feed you, guide you, and protect you?

Who We Belong To

It is a good thing to have a person in your life who looks out for your well-being. It may be a parent, a spouse, or even a good friend. However, I want you to allow your spirit to embrace this truth—the *Lord* is *my Shepherd*! My mother did a wonderful job in raising me along with my brother and sisters. There were seven of us, and I'm sure it was not easy finding a way to provide for all those children. I know that she did the best she could to nourish and protect us. There were times, however, when she wanted to do more for us but due to limited means was simply unable to do so. I am also sure that when her own limited resources ran out she would look to her Good Shepherd. What does it mean to have the Lord as your shepherd?

First, you are acknowledging that God, the supreme Creator of the heavens and earth, is your shepherd. "Pastor Warren, are you suggesting that the God who created everything and who owns everything is the one responsible for taking care of me?" I am not suggesting, but *emphatically* declaring to you that the *Lord* is your shepherd and He is everything you need!

> *The earth is the Lord's, and the fulness thereof; the world, and they that dwell therein* (Psalm 24:1).

God has revealed Himself to us through His various names.

- God is my Shepherd (supreme creator).

- *Yahweh* is my Shepherd (the great *I am*).
- *Elohim* is my Shepherd (God of gods).
- *Adonai* is my Shepherd (the Master and Lord of all).
- *Jehovah-Hoseenu* is my sheperd (the Lord who is my maker).
- *El-Shaddai* is my Shepherd (God who is mighty to nourish).
- *Jehovah-Rohi* is my Shepherd (the Lord who is my Shepherd).
- *Jehovah-Rophe* is my Shepherd (the Lord who is my Healer).
- *Jehovah-Shalom* is my Shepherd (the Lord my Peace).
- *Jehovah-Shammah* is my Shepherd (the Lord is there with me).
- *Jehovah-Tsidkenu* is my Shepherd (the Lord my Righteousness).
- *Jehovah-Nissi* is my Shepherd (the Lord my Banner).
- *Jehovah-Jireh* is my Shepherd (the Lord who sees to the need).

Do you see the picture of the One who is responsible for your well-being?

I have observed how the children of the rich and the famous carry themselves. They walk and talk with a certain air about them. It is something inherent in them, not because of what they have done or accomplished, but because of *who* they belong to. I can even remember watching the dog of a certain wealthy family strut around the house with a certain air about him. *Even the dog knew who he belonged to!*

I can't imagine any of those rich kids sitting up late at night, wringing their hands, worrying about where their next meal is coming from. They are not stressed out over how the mortgage payment is going to be made. They might not know how much their parents are worth, but they *do* know who they belong to and they trust them!

Years ago I heard this true story told by one of my former pastors. There was a poor lady living on the streets in a large, urban city. Her days consisted of scrounging around in garbage cans, looking for food that others had discarded, and begging passersby for money. She had no family to turn to and had lost contact with most of her former friends and neighbors. To make matters worse, her health was beginning to fail and she was showing early signs of dementia. As bad as this woman's plight had become, I have not gotten to the real tragedy of her story!

As it turns out, the woman was *not* poor after all! A wealthy relative had left a sizable amount of money in an account for the woman when she was a little girl. Over the years, through the miracle of compound interest, this account had grown to a staggering *363,000 dollars!*

Even in today's inflated society, that is a large sum of money, particularly for someone living in abject poverty.

Unfortunately, the woman didn't *know* the money existed! She had no idea what her actual net worth was. The woman could have been enjoying a wonderful lifestyle and getting the medical care she needed. Instead, she was suffering because she didn't know who she was or what she had.

> *My people are destroyed for lack of knowledge: because thou hast rejected knowledge, I will also reject thee, that thou shall be no priest to Me: seeing thou hast forgotten the law of thy God, I will also forget thy children* (Hosea 4:6).

Imagine if someone was to go to this woman and tell her about the money she had in the bank. I'm sure her life would change, because she now *knows* the truth. Unfortunately, there are people who get so used to living in bad conditions, they wouldn't know what to do if their fortunes changed. Their situation has become a way of life.

God wants His children to live according to *His* standards, not ours. It is time for every child of God to understand that having the Lord as your shepherd means you have a *birthright* to walk with your head up and to expect to live as only a child of God can. The Lord is my Shepherd!

What Makes a True Shepherd?

Let us now take a look at what it means to be a shepherd. Webster's dictionary defines a *shepherd* as "one who tends sheep; one who watches over and guides a flock."[1] A typical Bedouin (Middle Eastern, nomadic) shepherd led his flock from one water hole to another and one pasture to another. The relationship between the shepherd and his flock is similar to the relationship between the pastor and his church. We will examine the latter relationship in a later chapter.

Hebrews 13:20 refers to the Lord Jesus as the *Great Shepherd,* and in First Peter 5:4 the Lord is called the *Chief Shepherd*. In John 10:11, Jesus identifies Himself as the *Good Shepherd* and explains to His disciples the difference between a true shepherd and a false one. The false shepherd is a hireling. What are the characteristics of the hireling? First, the hireling doesn't actually know the sheep. He is only there to benefit himself. Secondly, instead of feeding the sheep, the hireling robs the sheep by fleecing them of their wool. In addition, since the false shepherd (hireling) does not have a real relationship with the sheep, he turns and runs when the wolf or some other predator attacks the flock.

Unfortunately, there are far too many hirelings that masquerade as true shepherds over the flock of God today. Jesus, in fact, identifies satan as a thief and a false shepherd because he only comes to steal, kill, and destroy (see John 10:10).

On the other hand, Jesus clearly identifies the nature of a true shepherd. A true shepherd must *know* his flock. A true shepherd can identify each of his sheep by name and personal character traits. Also, the sheep will know the voice of a true shepherd.

> *But he that entereth in by the door is the shepherd of the sheep. To him the porter openeth; and the sheep hear his voice: and he calleth his own sheep by name, and leadeth them out. And when he putteth forth his own sheep, he goeth before them, and the sheep follow him: for they know his voice. And a stranger will they not follow, but will flee from him: for they know not the voice of strangers* (John 10:2-5).

There are three chief responsibilities of a true shepherd. The shepherd must perform these three duties. If he does not consistently do these things, the sheep will wander off and eventually die of hunger and thirst or, worse yet, be devoured by predators. The three responsibilities are:

- The shepherd must *feed* the flock.
- The shepherd must *lead* the flock.
- The shepherd must *protect* the flock.

Feed, lead, and protect. In other words, the true shepherd is responsible for the total welfare of his sheep. Remember, the Lord is your Shepherd. We will examine these three duties of a true shepherd in a later chapter.

First, I want to explain something very *powerful* that Jesus reveals in John 10.

> ***I am** the door: by Me if any man enter in, he shall be saved, and shall go in and out, and find pasture. The thief cometh not, but for to steal, and to kill, and to destroy: I am come that they might have life, and that they might have it more abundantly. **I am** the good shepherd: the good shepherd giveth His life for the sheep* (John 10:9-11).

In verses 9 and 11 Jesus refers to Himself using the covenant name of God. "*I am the door*" and "*I am the good shepherd.*" In John 6 Jesus declares "*I am the bread of life*" on three different occasions while talking to a group of followers in the city of Capernaum (see John 6:35,48,51). Most of Jesus' followers at this time were Jewish and they understood the assertion He was making by using the covenant name *I am.* This claim upset His disciples so much that many of them turned away from Him and no longer followed Him. The next time Jesus uses this phrase is found in John chapter 8. The scribes and Pharisees had confronted Jesus with a woman who had been caught in the act of adultery. They wanted Jesus to condemn the woman according to Mosaic Law (see John 8:3-12). Jesus refused to condemn the woman, choosing rather to forgive her and charging her to go and sin no more. He then declares: "***I am** the light of the world*" (John 8:12). After the religious leaders repeatedly challenged Jesus on His right to use this covenant name, He finally came out and plainly stated *"Verily, verily, I say unto you, Before Abraham was, **I am**"* (John 8:58).

The people were so angry at Jesus for saying this that they took up stones to kill Him! Why did this phrase upset the people? The people of Jesus' day, especially the religious leaders, understood very clearly what Jesus was asserting by using the covenant name *I am*. From their study of the books of Moses, their law, as well as the books of the prophets, they knew that this was the name God revealed Himself as. In Genesis chapter 15, God revealed Himself to Abram using His covenant name for the first time.

> *After these things the word of the Lord came unto Abram in a vision, saying, Fear not, Abram: **I am** thy shield, and thy exceeding great reward* (Genesis 15:1).

In revealing Himself to Abram using the covenant name *I am*, God was literally *prophesying* to Abram. Let me explain. Whatever God *does*, He *says* first! When God created the heavens and the earth, He said it first. We have a record of the things God has said in this earth. We call this record the Bible, or the Word of God. However, God's spoken Word, or the *logos*, is not just a record of what God has said. God's Word is *alive* with the very nature of God. God's living Word, or *Rhema*, supersedes all other realities and circumstances. In other words, no matter what your present circumstances are, the Living Word of God (*Rhema*) will supersede and change the situation!

God visits Abram a second time in Genesis chapter 17 and again reveals Himself to Abram as *I am*, the Almighty God. However, this time God also speaks a *Rhema* word directly to Abram that would ultimately change his life. In order to establish His covenant between Abram and Himself, God speaks these words to Abram:

> *As for me, behold, My covenant is with thee, and thou shalt be a father of many nations. Neither shall thy name any more be called Abram, but thy name shall be Abraham; for a father of many nations have I made thee* (Genesis 17:4-5).

The name Abram translates to "a high or respected father." The name Abraham, on the other hand, means "a father of a multitude." Think about the significance of this. At the time this *Rhema* word was spoken to Abram, he did not have *any* children by his wife, Sarai (Sarah). His only son, Ishmael, had been born to Sarai's Egyptian handmaiden 13 years earlier (see Gen. 16:15). Yet God comes to Abram and declares that he is a father of a *multitude!*

Imagine Abraham traveling throughout Mesopotamia and introducing himself as "Abraham." There were probably a few chuckles from the strangers Abraham met when he told them his name. Remember, during that time, having many sons gave you power and prestige in your region. So when God changed Abram's name to Abraham, He was actually speaking (prophesying) to his circumstance. Every time Abraham spoke his name, he was acknowledging God's *Rhema* Word in his life. Every time Abraham spoke his name, he was bringing the creative power of Almighty God to bear on his natural circumstances.

The *natural* circumstances said Abraham was 99 years old and no longer had the strength to father a child. The *natural* circumstances said Sarah was 90 years old and past her child-bearing years. Fortunately, God is not bound by your natural circumstances. And, through God's living Word, *you* are not bound by your natural circumstances either! According to Romans chapter 4, Abraham's faith in what God had *said* gave him the strength to produce a son when he was 100 years old! Abraham refused to allow his *natural* circumstances to limit the *supernatural* power of God's Word.

Remember, faith in God's Word does not demand that you pretend your circumstances don't exist. Faith in God's Word *does* demand that we call those things that are not seen yet as if they already exist (see Rom. 4:17). When you *say* what God has *said*, you bring the power of God's living Word to bear upon your circumstances! Never hesitate to declare what God has already declared over your life. It may seem foolish to someone else, but the results will speak for themselves. The *Lord* is my *Shepherd*, I shall not want. Say it when you don't have anything. Say it when you have lost everything. Say it when everyone around you is laughing at you. Say it when your goals seem far away. Say it because it is *true!*

> *It is the spirit that quickeneth; the flesh profiteth nothing: the* ***words*** *that I speak unto you,* ***they are spirit****, and* ***they are life*** (John 6:63).

Your True Shepherd

In Exodus chapter 3, we find the occasion where God calls Moses while he is tending to his father-in-law, Jethro's, flock of sheep on the back side of the mountain, Horeb. While there, God speaks to Moses out of a burning bush that was not consumed. Moses is instructed by God to go to Pharaoh, king of Egypt, and to bring the children of Israel out of the land of Egypt. Moses protests this calling at first, saying he is inadequate for the job, but then finally submits to God's request. He then asks God who he should say sent him when they ask for His name.

> *And God said unto Moses,* ***I AM THAT I AM:*** *and He said, Thus shalt thou say unto the children of Israel,* ***I AM*** *hath sent me unto you* (Exodus 3:14).

God went on to say that this name would be a memorial throughout all generations, as a token of God's covenant-keeping power to His children. So when Jesus invokes this name, *I am*, the people clearly understood what He meant. Jesus was letting them know that He is all they need and that He will keep covenant with them also. The Lord is saying, "I am the true shepherd and not a hireling. I will not run out on you when things get difficult. I will *feed* you, *lead* you, and *protect* you!"

Think of it, dear child of God. The great *I am* is your shepherd. Your great shepherd is saying to you, "Whatever you need Me to be, *I am*."

- Do you need protection? The Good Shepherd is your shield.
- Do you need healing? The Good Shepherd is your physician.
- Do you need forgiveness? The Good Shepherd is your righteousness.
- Do you need food? The Good Shepherd will see to your need.
- Do you need guidance? The Good Shepherd is the Way, Truth, and Life.
- Do you need a friend? The Good Shepherd is always there.

Who is he that can harm you when the Lord is your shepherd? Jesus said the Good Shepherd would lay down His life for the sheep. In other words, the Good Shepherd would sacrifice His own life before letting anything or anyone harm you. The Lord has a place of safety and protection right here for you *now*. You can continue to be overwhelmed by your present circumstances, or you can choose to live under the security of the great *I am!* When difficult times arise, God has a secret place where you can enter in and find everything you need in this life (see Ps. 27:1,5)

Whisper these words in your spirit: *The Lord is my shepherd; I shall not want.*

Endnote

1. *Webster's Ninth New Collegiate Dictionary* (Springfield, MA: Merriam-Webster, 1991), s.v. "Shepherd."

CHAPTER 2

He Makes Me Lie Down

(EL-SHADDAI)
GOD WHO IS MIGHTY TO NOURISH

One of the most challenging responsibilities of the shepherd is to find good pasture for the sheep to graze in. Sometimes it was necessary for the shepherd to lead the flock from one area to another because a watering hole might have dried up or a pasture might become barren. The spring rains would have produced good feeding for a while. However, several months out of each year the shepherd would have to guide the sheep over long distances and rough terrain in search of suitable feeding ground. As a result, sheep needed constant protection from wild animals that would follow and attack the flock.

Made Full and Content

Have you ever wondered why God likens His people to sheep? A study in the Word gives us valuable insight into the nature of sheep. Several facts about the nature of sheep will help us understand why God compares us most often to sheep. First, unlike cattle, sheep must be *led*, not driven.

> *To him the porter openeth; and the sheep hear his voice: and he calleth his own sheep by name, and* ***leadeth*** *them out. And when he putteth forth his own sheep, he goeth before them, and the sheep follow him: for they know his voice* (John 10:3-4).

Sheep will instinctively follow their own shepherd because they know and trust him. Time and relationship have taught them that their shepherd will always provide for them. It is much easier to stay on course when you have a good leader in front of you. This is true whether in your family, job, church, or country. This truth is vital for sheep because of their *inherent nature* to go astray. If you had a whole flock of sheep but no shepherd to guide them, most of them would panic and become confused. In this frightened state, they would begin to wander off in different directions.

> *All we like sheep have gone astray; we have turned every one to his own way; and the Lord hath laid on Him the iniquity of us all* (Isaiah 53:6).

This is why it is vitally important that you have a good shepherd watching over you. This is also why the good shepherd must always put the interest of the sheep ahead of his own self-interest.

Given this nature of sheep, it is important that the sheep remain at ease in order for them to properly graze and be satisfied. Remember, one of the primary responsibilities of the shepherd is to feed the sheep. In fact, it is when the sheep are feeding undisturbed that they are the most valuable to their owner. A well-fed sheep will be nice and fat, with a thick, rich layer of wool on its body. A poor, thin, emaciated flock would be a bad reflection on the shepherd. Let me show you what David meant by this verse and what wonderful things God has for you.

*He **maketh** me lie to down in green pastures.* When conditions are right, sheep will graze from very early in the morning until just before noon. They will then lie down for several hours and rest. As the sheep are resting, they are *chewing the cud.* Simply put, this means they are bringing up their food in order to chew it again. This process allows the sheep to fatten up and put on more wool. The greener the grass, the more content and healthy the sheep are going to be.

I remember driving through the Appalachian Mountains in Virginia several years ago. As I was riding I saw a large flock of sheep grazing in a field. What caught my attention is that every one of the sheep was standing upright in one place as they grazed. Not *one* sheep was lying down in the field. It was interesting to see when I drove by the same field on my way back several hours later, I noticed that all the sheep were still standing in basically the same spot. None of them were lying down yet. I later found out why.

Sheep will not lie down until they are *full* and *content!*

He *makes* me lie down in green pastures. I want you to fully grasp what the Lord is saying to you. God has compared us to sheep, which by their nature will not lie down until they are completely full. And yet our Good Shepherd said He would *make* (force, compel) us to lie down. This means we are content and full!

> *Blessed be the Lord, who daily loadeth us with benefits, even the God of our salvation.* ***Selah*** (Psalm 68:19).

Notice God loads us up with His benefits every day. This means we don't have to worry about tomorrow. We can enjoy what God has for us today. In fact, Jesus specifically instructs us not to worry about tomorrow. First, worrying about tomorrow will not accomplish anything. No one has ever solved a problem simply by worrying about it. Second, worry, anxiety, and stress can lead to serious physical and mental health issues. Jesus taught a simple yet powerful truth to His disciples—you are more important to your heavenly Father than all the lilies of the valley and all the fowl of the air. If God takes special care of these small parts of His creation, how much more will He provide for His children?

> *Therefore I say unto you, Take no thought for your life, what ye shall eat, or what ye shall drink; nor yet for your body, what ye shall*

put on. Is not the life more than meat, and the body than raiment? ...Which of you by taking thought can add one cubit unto his stature? (Matthew 6:25,27)

The phrase *take no thought* literally means "do not be anxious or worried." Jesus is not advocating that we make no preparations for our families and our future. Wise planning and hard work will almost always lead to success. However, Jesus makes it clear that worry and anxiety will *never* change your circumstances for the better. How many of you have worried your debt away? Has anxiety contributed to your bank account? Have you been able to worry your illness away? On the contrary, worry and stress have probably made these things worse. Some of you worry so much that if you stopped worrying, you wouldn't know what else to think about!

You need to replace that stinking thinking with good thoughts from your Good Shepherd. In Matthew chapter 6 Jesus further instructed His disciples to *not* worry about what they were going to eat or drink or what clothes they were going to wear. The Lord pointed out that those were the things that the people who did not have a good shepherd spent all their time seeking after.

But seek ye first the kingdom of God, and His righteousness; and all these things shall be added unto you (Matthew 6:33).

Notice that all these things (what I eat, drink, and wear) shall be *added* to me. This means they are in addition to something else that I am already receiving from the Lord! When the Lord is your Shepherd you should never have to worry about your basic needs in life. God takes care of His children. If the Lord feeds the little sparrow and clothes the lilies of the field, *how much more* will He provide for you! David blessed the Lord for all the many benefits God had provided for him.

> *Bless the Lord, O my soul: and all that is within me, bless His holy name. Bless the Lord, O my soul, and forget not all His benefits* (Psalm 103:1-2).

What were the benefits David sang and wrote about in this Psalm?

> *Who forgiveth* ***all*** *thine iniquities; who healeth* ***all*** *thy diseases; who redeemeth thy life from destruction; who crowneth thee with lovingkindness and tender mercies; who satisfieth thy mouth with good things; so that thy youth is renewed like the eagle's* (Psalm 103:3-5).

Let me show you another powerful nugget of truth that is found in this verse of Psalm 23. Sheep will *continue* to eat *until* they are full. As they continue eating, they will sometimes begin to tilt. Because of the shape of their bodies, once full they will actually fall over and *lie down* in the field! Now consider what the Lord is revealing to you in this text.

He *makes* me lie down in green pastures. Your Good Shepherd won't stop feeding you until you are completely full and satisfied.

Notice one more thing. The pasture is *still* full of green grass. The Good Shepherd will feed you so well you will be forced to lie down in the field while there is *still* abundance all around you! You haven't seen God's best for your life yet. Let the Lord be your source of nourishment instead of trying to find things that will satisfy you. Feeding from the table of the Lord (the Word) will bring the peace and satisfaction you are searching for today.

> *Great peace have they which love Thy law: and nothing shall offend them* (Psalm 119:165).

Feeding the Sheep

Let me at this time take a moment to speak to the pastors who shepherd the flock of God. There is no greater calling in this life than to be a shepherd of God's people. After more than 35 years in active ministry in churches, prisons, and schools, I am still humbled by the fact that the Lord has allowed me the awesome privilege of sharing His powerful, life-changing Word with thousands of people. And while I have enjoyed being a pastor, educator, and counselor, I constantly remind myself of the seriousness of the calling. We must always remember that the sole reason for this calling is to feed, lead, and protect the sheep.

In John 21, Jesus met with His disciples after His resurrection on the coast of the sea of Tiberias. After Jesus' crucifixion, the disciples had gone back to their jobs as fishermen. When the disciples came back to the shore, Jesus roasted some of the fish they had caught and they all sat down and dined together. At that time, Jesus charged the apostle Peter with the most important responsibility he would have as the leader of the new, soon-to-be fledgling Church. Jesus asked Peter if he loved Him more than his career as a fisherman. When Peter answered in the affirmative, Jesus emphatically instructed him to *feed His sheep* (see John 21:15).

Jesus repeated the question two more times. Each time Peter responded that he loved the Lord. To which Jesus replied—*feed My sheep*. Jesus considered this charge so important that He stated it three times. If ever there was a time when people needed to hear a clear, strong word from the prophets and servants God, it is now! If you are an apostle, prophet, evangelist, pastor, or teacher, you share this charge with Peter and all those ministers who have come before you.

> *And He* [Jesus] *gave some, apostles; and some, prophets; and some, evangelists; and some, pastors and teachers; for the perfecting of the saints, for the work of the ministry, for the edifying of the body of Christ* (Ephesians 4:11-12).

It is the job of the pastor (mainly) to feed the sheep on good green grass. This good green grass is the Word of God. The Word will help the sheep grow into spiritual maturity. The result will be a strong, knowledgeable person who is not easily deceived by every new fad and doctrine that comes out.

A study of the Word reveals that God has reserved severe judgment for those shepherds who will not feed the sheep. The Old Testament is replete with examples of woe and judgment being pronounced upon the prophets of Israel who refused to fulfill their obligation to feed the people of God. One such pronouncement came from the prophet Jeremiah:

> *Woe be unto the pastors that destroy and scatter the sheep of My pasture! saith the Lord. Therefore thus saith the Lord God of Israel against the pastors that feed My people; Ye have scattered My flock, and driven them away, and have not visited them: behold, I will visit upon you the evil of your doings, saith the Lord* (Jeremiah 23:1-2).

This reminds me of some words from a song we used to sing in church when I was a teenager.

> Fill my cup, Lord, I lift it up, Lord,
> Come and quench this thirsting in my soul
> Bread of Heaven, feed me till I want no more
> Fill my cup, fill it up and make me whole.[1]

The Word of God will replace the fear and disappointments we have had in our lives. Let God fill the void in your heart. There is no substitute for peace of mind and contentment. When your mind is troubled and your spirit is disquieted, you wouldn't go and hug your house or your car. It's time to get rid of the stress, anger, and resentment that has built up in you and begin to feed on the green grass God has for you until you just tilt over and fall into God's abundance. In the midst of the confusion around us, God's Word will provide you with strength, direction, and purpose. You will not only survive but thrive. In fact, you will have enough to share with others in your family and community who are hurting. Take what God has given you and make a positive impact on your community.

Endnote

1. Richard Blanchard, "Fill My Cup, Lord," 1964.

Chapter 3

Still Waters Run Deep

(Jehovah-Shalom)
The Lord My Peace

In the previous chapter, I mentioned the fact that sheep tend to lie down only when they are full. Another little-known fact about sheep is they will only drink from still, calm water. A good shepherd knows that sheep will not drink from disturbed, running water. Because of the timid nature of the sheep, they will wait until the water is relatively still and calm before they drink. David, the shepherd, knew that it was not only his responsibility to feed the sheep but to also find a calm reservoir of water to refresh and strengthen them. The prophet Isaiah speaks to the nature of sheep:

> *All we like sheep have gone astray; we have turned every one to his own way; and the Lord hath laid on Him the iniquity of us all. He was oppressed, and He was afflicted, yet He* ***opened***

> ***not His mouth:*** *He is brought as a lamb, to the slaughter, and as a* ***sheep before her shearers is dumb,*** *so He openeth not His mouth* (Isaiah 53:6-7).

A farmer once told me that if you take a pig to the slaughter house the pig will sense that its end is near. The pig will resist you and squirm and squeal all the way to the end. I can imagine the pig saying, "You might get your ham, but I'm not going quietly!" Unlike the pig to the slaughter, the sheep will go quietly to be sheared, seemingly unaware of what's about to take place. The sheep will even stand there as its wool is sheared off. This messianic prophecy found its fulfillment in the ministry of Jesus Christ. As Christ stood before King Herod and later before Pontius Pilate, He would not open His mouth in His defense even when faced with the threat of death. Pontius Pilate became so frustrated when questioning Jesus that he threatened Jesus with execution if He did not respond to his queries. Pilate was under the false impression that he, not God the Father, held the Lord's fate in his hand (see John 19:9-10). Jesus was simply displaying the true nature of a sheep because He trusted in His heavenly Father.

This quiet nature of sheep makes it necessary for the shepherd to find quiet water. The quiet water represents the peace God has for us. If someone today could create a pill or a drink that gave peace, that person would become the greatest, wealthiest human on the planet! Most people would be willing to part with all their worldly possessions in exchange for a lasting peace. What would you do for personal peace? I'm not talking about a feeling of happiness. You can manufacture or even buy fun and happiness. You can surround yourself with happy people and do all sorts of fun things. Some people try to make themselves "feel" happy by almost any means. However, I'm talking about the peace of God. This peace is a deep-rooted, quiet assurance way down in the soul that will keep you steady and focused when all "hell" has broken loose around you! God's peace goes beyond anything man can produce on his own.

> *Rejoice in the Lord always: and again I say, Rejoice. Let your moderation be known unto all men. The Lord is at hand. Be careful for nothing; but in every thing by prayer and supplication with thanksgiving let your requests be made known unto God. And* ***the peace of God, which passeth all understanding,*** *shall keep your hearts and minds through Christ Jesus* (Philippians 4:4-7).

What kind of peace surpasses understanding? The kind of peace you have, when *you* don't understand why you still have it! There are some situations we will find ourselves in when we really should have fallen apart. And yet we are able to hold it together. Why? The peace of God. I hear people talk about going on a search to "find" themselves. Unfortunately, some of you might not like what you see when you "find" yourself. Which of these two passages describe your present situation?

Great peace have they which love Thy law: and nothing shall offend them (Psalm 119:165).

The wicked are like the troubled sea, when it cannot rest, whose waters cast up mire and dirt (Isaiah 57:20).

We cannot really experience the kind of calm and quiet in our hearts that God intended for us until we let the Good Shepherd lead us to the still waters. Think of what this can do for your spiritual, physical, and mental well-being. Also, imagine the impact this kind of peace will have on our relationships. Many of the arguments we get into with loved ones very often stem from some dissatisfaction or anger we harbor within our hearts. To gain some relief from this internal strife, we unload on the people who are closest to us. Before long, everyone is walking around on eggshells, grumbling at each other. I Googled the words "*peace*" and "*song*" and discovered that there are over *50 million* references to these words! It seems the whole world is searching for this elusive commodity.

Step Out in Faith

In Matthew 14, we find the account of Jesus feeding the multitude with only five loaves of bread and two fishes. There are two things in this chapter that happened after this miraculous event that I want us to examine. First, Jesus sent His disciples on a boat to the other side of the sea while He went up into a mountain to pray. After spending some quiet, quality time in prayer with His heavenly Father, Jesus headed across the sea, walking on the water! Meanwhile, the disciples were stuck in the middle of the sea being tossed around by a violent sea. The text refers to this storm as a *contrary wind.*

So here we have the disciples stuck in the middle of the sea, scared to death. Many of these men were fishermen, and they knew these waters very well. Nevertheless, they couldn't make any headway with this contrary wind in spite of their best efforts. It appeared they were not getting any closer to their destination on the other side. When things looked like they couldn't get any worse, they see what appears to be a ghost out in the water heading straight for the boat! However, what appeared to be a ghost was none other than Jesus, walking on the water.

As He approached the boat, Jesus cried out to the disciples, *"Be of good cheer; it is I; be not afraid"* (Matt. 14:27). Upon hearing these words, Peter responded by saying, "If it's You, Lord, then bid me come to You." Peter's request implied a level of faith and trust in the Lord since the only way to get to Jesus was by stepping *out* of the boat and walking on the water. Jesus responded with a simple command—*come.* In other words, Jesus ordered Peter to get out of the boat and walk across the water toward Him. Peter obeyed the command and stepped out of the boat!

A beautiful thing took place at that time. In the middle of the sea, with a contrary wind blowing, Peter began to walk on water! Imagine, if you will, the spectacle of this scene! In the middle of the night, while a turbulent sea was raging, two men defied the laws of nature and walked on water! This would have been an outstanding miracle even if it had been a clear, sunny day. However, under the circumstances, what happened defied all human explanation.

Unfortunately, Peter was distracted by the boisterous wind and became afraid. As a result, he began to sink. Notice, however, that as soon as he began to sink he cried out to the Lord, and Jesus immediately stretched out His hand and caught him. This would suggest that Peter was much closer to the Lord than he thought. The Good Shepherd is *always* closer to us than we think. He is *Jehovah Shammah* (I am God who is present).

Whenever you trust the voice of the Good Shepherd enough to step out of the boat and get into the water, He will be right there beside you. I have heard ministers criticize Peter for allowing himself to be distracted by the wind and not focusing on the Lord. It is true that Peter became afraid by allowing the circumstances (the contrary wind) to distract him. It's not as if he could have walked on the water had it been a clear, windless, sunny day!

How often have we stepped out on faith to do something bold, only to retreat in the face of a *contrary wind?* How many times have you found yourself in the middle of a bad situation while trying to reach your goals on the other side? To make matters worse, there is a contrary wind blowing in your face which is keeping you from making any progress. It might be a contrary wind of financial debt, physical illness, depression, marital problems, unforgiveness, or a host of other issues. Sometimes, the contrary wind may even come from the people who are closest to you. Do not let people or your circumstances keep you from stepping out by faith and walking on the water. Your miracle may be *outside* the boat! If the Lord is beckoning you to step out of the boat, don't hesitate to obey the command.

Remember, the Good Shepherd is right there beside you, and He will never let you sink when you step out by faith. God can handle our mistakes. I heard it put this way: "Faith let Peter walk on water, but mercy wouldn't let him drown!" Consider this—if the Lord hasn't gotten *on board your boat* and you aren't making any progress toward achieving your goals, it might be time for you to *get off the boat* and go to the Lord! In order to make this bold step of faith, however, you must trust the Good Shepherd enough to take a risk.

Peace Outside the Boat

The word *entrepreneur* is a French term which literally means "The one who assumes the risk." Many of you want to achieve great things, but you are unwilling to take the risk and step out on the Word of the Lord. The Good Shepherd will always say "come." Think about this powerful statement: You will find *more peace* out on the water with the Lord than sitting on the boat with a bunch of people who are scared and unwilling to take any action. In fact, taking the risk and stepping out of the boat might have been the safest thing for Peter to do. Imagine for a moment what the other disciples on the boat were thinking at this time. Remember, they were all afraid and thought the figure approaching the boat was a ghost. These are some of the things I can imagine they were saying to Peter as he stepped out of the boat.

- There's a ghost out there, Peter.
- It's too windy, Peter.
- Why don't you wait for the storm to die down, Peter?
- You're going to sink, Peter.
- You can't walk on water, Peter.
- Let's all stay together, Peter.

Ever heard these statements before? They all come from well-meaning people. The Lord is looking for people who are willing to take the risk and step out on His Word. Remember, a miracle is only a miracle from *our* perspective. When God performs a miracle, He's just doing what God does! In other words, what we call a miracle is the normal realm in which God operates all the time. That is exactly what God wants His people to experience.

> *For the eyes of the Lord run to and fro throughout the whole earth, to shew Himself strong in*

the behalf of them whose heart is perfect toward Him... (2 Chronicles 16:9).

The Lord is actually *looking* for someone who is willing to step out on the water, no matter how crazy it might seem to others. In other words, God wants you to let Him do what God does best! What God does best is exceed what we can do through our own human abilities. Faith in God's Word brings the power of God to bear upon any and every situation you are dealing with. In fact, God will move Heaven and earth when He finds someone who will dare to believe His Word. Consider this—God *lives* in the realm of the supernatural. Miracles are the order of the day. When Jesus was here on earth, He performed miracles practically every day. The Lord would go to a city or town to teach the people, and before long everyone who was sick or diseased would show up. The Lord would not send the folks home until He had healed them all! Miracles followed the Lord everywhere He went. You would think that it would be extremely hard to impress the Lord with anything that we could do, but we can.

There was an incident recorded in the Gospel of Matthew where a man, who was not even one of the so-called "chosen" people, actually did something that *astounded* the Lord. In Matthew 8, Jesus had just healed a man who had been stricken with the dreadful disease of leprosy. As He entered into the town of Capernaum, a centurion (an officer who commanded 100 Roman soldiers) approached Him and petitioned the Lord to heal his servant who was at home sick with the disease of palsy. Jesus agreed to come to the man's home and heal his servant. However, the centurion felt he was not worthy of the Lord entering his home. So he asks the Lord to just *"speak the word only"* and his servant would be healed. This demonstration of faith absolutely astounded the Lord!

> *The centurion answered and said, Lord, I am not worthy that Thou shouldest come under my roof: but speak the word only, and my servant shall be healed. ...When Jesus heard it, He* ***marvelled****, and said to them that followed, Verily I say unto you, I have not found so* ***great faith****, no, not in Israel* (Matthew 8:8,10).

Do you want to see God's miracle-working power? Do you need God to move in your situation? God is looking for someone who will step out of the realm of the ordinary and, at His command, step into the realm of the extraordinary! Remember, it is calmer and safer out of the boat *with* the Lord than being in the boat *without* Him.

The peace you and I are looking for can only be found in the Lord. And if the Lord is there with you, it won't matter whether you are in the boat or on the water. It could be a perfectly sunny, beautiful day or stormy seas with a contrary wind blowing in your face. The Lord will steer you into the peaceful harbor. You may have to go through the storm, but you won't stay there. Notice that when Jesus and Peter got on the boat the contrary wind immediately stopped.

Living in His Presence

In order for us to exercise this kind of faith in the Lord, we must spend time in His presence. It will be much easier for us to trust the word of our Good Shepherd when we are familiar with His voice. It is imperative that you take the time to refresh your soul by spending time with God. Remember, in Matthew 14 the reason Jesus was not on the boat with the disciples was because He needed to get away from the crowd and spend some quiet time in prayer. Jesus had just finished a very successful crusade. He had taught thousands of His disciples and healed many of them of their diseases. The Lord had also fed a multitude with a few fish and several loaves of bread. Yet after all these positive things, the Lord found it necessary to steal away and refresh Himself by spending quiet time in prayer.

> *Thou wilt keep him in* ***perfect peace****, whose mind is stayed on Thee: because he trusteth in Thee. Trust ye in the Lord for ever: for in the Lord Jehovah is everlasting strength* (Isaiah 26:3-4).

I remember when the Lord led me to establish the Word and Faith Fellowship Church. I was still working in my secular job as a claims authorizer for the Social Security Administration in Baltimore, Maryland. My wife and I, along with our two small children, started conducting church services in the basement of our home with five other members. As the small congregation grew, we were no longer able to hold our services in the basement and soon began to look for a church building. After a six weeks' search, we found a building in an impoverished section of town that was occupied at the time by another church. The congregation of this church had dwindled down to about five souls, and the pastor was no longer able to make the mortgage payment on the property.

At that time our own congregation had grown to about 50 members. We knew that God wanted us to move into that building and that He would provide the necessary funds to make it happen. There were only a handful of working men in the church at that time. The rest of the congregation was comprised mainly of young mothers with little children and elderly people on fixed incomes. In fact, I was the single largest contributor in the church, accounting for about 40 percent of all the weekly receipts. When I inquired about buying the building, I was put in contact with an elderly Jewish gentleman who agreed to meet with me at one of the local delicatessens.

The man took one look at me and decided he was not going to deal with me. Apparently, he had sized me up and determined that I was not going to be able to make the deal. The selling price of the building was only 39,000 dollars. However, based on what we had, it may as well have been 39 million dollars. We had 50 dollars in the church's bank account and were averaging about 450 dollars a week in offerings.

When I asked the gentleman why he didn't want to sell the building to me, he looked me in the eyes and said, "I know your type. You probably mean well, but I know that you're not going to keep up with the payments, just like the preacher before you. The only way you're going to get that building is to pay me cash money for it right now."

When I heard these words, the Spirit of God rose up within my spirit and said, "How dare he limit what I can do for one of My children!"

I immediately blurted out, "How much time will you give me to get your money?"

He said, "I'll give you thirty days, but it won't matter because I know you can't do it."

He was actually right, because I couldn't do it. However, my faith wasn't in me, but in my God. In *17 days*, after much prayer, I put 39,000 dollars in the man's hand and we took possession of our first church building! Since that time we have made several other purchases in the same way, by stepping out in faith. You *cannot* keep a faith-filled man (or woman) down! Once you step out in faith and put your trust in God, the *peace* of God will calm the storms within, even if the storms without are still raging.

> *Confess your faults one to another, and pray one for another, that ye may be healed. The* ***effectual fervent*** *prayer of a righteous man availeth much* (James 5:16).

How do you learn to walk and live in the peace of God? Remember, peace does not come from external sources. It is a quality and state of the soul that we experience as a result of being in a right relationship with God. Peace is listed as one of the fruit of the Spirit in Galatians 5. If you have accepted Jesus as Lord of your life, then the peace of God is already *within* you. You don't have to try and find it through some other source. Don't let external distractions rob you of your peace. In times of stress, draw from the reservoir of peace that is in you. If you don't have the peace of God in your heart, isn't it time to change that? Take a moment and pray this prayer:

Heavenly Father, I acknowledge that You are the true source of real peace. I thank You for providing my peace through the sacrifice of Jesus Christ. Cleanse me from all unrighteousness and fill me with Your Spirit. I receive Your peace into my heart now. I will not worry or be anxious about anything. But in all things I will pray and make my requests known unto You. Teach me to trust in my Good Shepherd. Thank You.

May the peace of God be with your spirit always. Amen.

Chapter 4

Restoration: He Restores My Soul

(Jehovah-Hoseenu) The Lord Who Is Maker

To *restore* means, "to return something or someone to its former state; to refresh, renew, heal, or cure."[1] In John 10, Jesus states not only that the sheep know the voice of the Good Shepherd but also that the Shepherd knows His sheep.

> *I am the good shepherd, and know My sheep, and am known of Mine* (John 10:14).

In many Middle Eastern regions, there are areas where sheep herding is the main occupation and a way of life. Some owners may have their own sheepfold containing thousands of sheep. Other shepherds with smaller flocks may share a common sheepfold with shepherds from the same village or town. Early in the morning, the shepherd would have to stand at the gate and call out his sheep. Each sheep would come out at the sound of his shepherd's voice, which he is familiar with. Once all his sheep are gathered together, he would lead them out in search of food and water.

This journey could sometimes take several hours. By midmorning on some days, the temperature could reach extreme levels. In addition, some of the mountainous regions made the journey difficult and exhausting for the shepherd as well as the sheep. Many of the sheep would sustain minor cuts and scrapes along the way. Others might incur more serious injuries such as a broken limb.

It was the shepherd's responsibility to tend to the wounds of his sheep. The shepherd would keep a constant eye out for any of the flock that needed to be ministered to. As the flock was grazing, those sheep that needed special care would be called out by the shepherd and taken care of.

Restoration

Caring for the sheep in many ways is very similar to raising children. Each of your children will have their own distinct personality and character traits. One child may be very aggressive while another child is shy. One may be sturdy and seldom get sick while another seems to stay sick all the time. As a good parent, you know how to deal with each of your children based on their individual needs and tendencies. A stern hand may be needed to keep the strong-willed child "in check." However, another child with a completely different personality would need a more gentle approach. The point is, all of them will need some comfort and personal care from you.

In like manner, the sheep would need some kind of attention from the shepherd. After being called by the shepherd, the sheep would come to him and receive *restoration*. This restoration might start with an examination of the sheep's ears, nose, hooves, and wool. The shepherd would be looking for cuts, scratches, or even small parasites that may have attached themselves to the sheep by burrowing into the ears or hooves. These things would be very irritating to the sheep and could cause sickness or disease if left untreated. The sheep actually looked forward to this interaction with the shepherd. This physical touching as well as the shepherd's gentle voice was comforting and therapeutic. After this restoration took place, the sheep were refreshed and able to continue the rest of the day's journey.

It is interesting that David, while writing Psalm 23, uses the word *soul* in this text. According to *The Expanded Vine's Expository Dictionary of New Testament Words*, the soul is the immaterial, invisible part of man. It is the seat of your personality as well as the seat of your will and purpose. The soul allows you to perceive, reflect, feel, and desire.[2]

During the course of our daily lives we often encounter challenges, hardships, afflictions, and even setbacks. Sometimes difficult decisions have to be made. For some the challenge could be dealing with a debilitating physical or emotional illness. Others may be dealing with a personal addiction or that of a family member. Many struggle with a mountain of financial debt. Still others are stressed out because of strained relationships with a spouse, a child, or a parent.

All these situations are in addition to the myriad of societal issues we are bombarded with every day. While many of these problems are caused by circumstances beyond our control, a few may be the result of our own lack of knowledge or poor choices. Even if we are fortunate enough not to have to deal with major crises, just the daily grind of tending to a family and working on a job makes *spiritual* and *emotional* restoration a daily necessity.

Begin With Repentance

The Book of Joel contains a message of judgment, repentance, and restoration. God had allowed the land of Palestine to be destroyed by a ravaging plague of locusts. As a result, the fields were stripped, the crops were eaten, and the harvest was wiped out. Remember, the people of Palestine were mainly an agrarian society at this time. As such, they were completely dependent on their crops for survival. Having their fields destroyed by a plague meant certain starvation and left them vulnerable to their enemies. In fact, the destruction was so thorough that restoration seemed impossible.

The prophet Joel makes it clear that those conditions existed because the people had turned away from God.

The prophet also told the people that they could turn the devastation around by humbling themselves before God through repentance.

To repent means to have a change of heart and to turn in a different direction. Joel warns the children of Israel that true repentance involves the rending or tearing of the heart. God was not interested in the people beating themselves physically or tearing up their garments. He also reminded them that if they truly did repent, God would be gracious to them and not only would forgive them but also would heal their land (see Joel 2:12-13).

When the people humbled themselves and repented as instructed, God heard them and restored the land. In fact, God promised to completely remove the plague from off the land and drive the locusts into the sea. God always responds to the soul which cries out to Him for mercy.

> *Then will the Lord be jealous for His land, and pity His people. Yea, the Lord will answer and say unto His people, Behold, I will send you corn, and wine, and oil, and ye shall be satisfied therewith: and I will no more make you a reproach among the heathen: ... Fear not, O land; be glad and rejoice: for the Lord will do great things* (Joel 2:18-19,21).

The key to turning your life, your family, and your nation around is to turn to God in repentance. Nothing moves the hand of God like a nation that will humble itself and repent and seek God's face. God instructed the children of Zion to be glad and rejoice because He was going to overflow their storehouses with crops and fill their vats with wine and oil. He would do this by sending the former and latter rains (the early and late rains) at the same time. God also told them that He would restore *all* the harvest that had been eaten up by the locust, the palmerworm, and the cankerworm.

Imagine the kind of turn around the children of God would experience by humbling themselves before God and turning from their wicked ways. They would go from total devastation of their crops to enjoying an abundance of food (see Joel 2:26).

We want *our circumstances* to turn around. But God wants *us* to turn around! True restoration must start in our hearts (souls). *He restores my soul.* Do you want to see your health restored? What about your family? Your finances? Your church? Your community? Wouldn't it be great to see our nation restored? Haven't you "had it up to here" with failure, discontent, and defeat? It seems all of society is collectively waiting for some relief and restoration. There is a way to turn around your family, church, community, and even the entire nation! God has outlined in His Word the steps we can follow in order to bring about revival and restoration. It is a very simple formula, but it gets right to the heart of the problem.

> *If I shut up heaven that there be no rain, or if I command the locusts to devour the land, or if I send pestilence among My people; if My people, which are called by My name, shall humble*

themselves, ***and*** *pray,* ***and*** *seek My face,* ***and*** *turn from their wicked ways;* ***then*** *will I hear from heaven, and will forgive their sin, and will* ***heal*** *their land* (2 Chronicles 7:13-14).

These two verses contain our prescription for restoration. Let's look at these steps in the order that God gives them to His people.

- The first thing we *must* do is *humble* ourselves; that is, we bow before a Holy God and acknowledge who He is.
- The next thing we do is *pray*. This prayer should include repentance and petition on behalf of our families and the nation.
- Next we *seek* God's face. We spend time in God's presence, seeking His will for our lives.
- Finally, we *turn* from our wicked ways. Now that we know His will for our lives, we begin to live according to His will.

The result will be God hearing us and sending His *healing* to our families and nation. The beauty of this plan is that it doesn't require everyone's participation to be effective. God only needs a few. The majority has never brought about positive change in any society. In fact, change usually starts with a small, committed group of people who are willing to make sacrifices in order to bring about change. Will you be one of the dedicated, committed persons who will do whatever it takes to see restoration take place? Your family and your country need you.

Buying Back

Another meaning for the word *restore* is "to recover from ruin and decay or to redeem." The word *redeem* reminds me of the old pawn shops that operated in my neighborhood years ago. When I was a boy, I remember seeing many families struggling to make ends meet. When things would get really bad, they would take their valuables such as diamond rings, watches, radios, and other electric appliances and "pawn" them. That is, they would give their valuables to the shop owner, known as the pawnbroker, in exchange for a certain amount of cash. This transaction was similar to a loan being made with the property being held as security. The pawnbroker would also give the person a ticket that would allow him to *redeem*, that is to *buy back*, his property at a future date.

There were two problems with this transaction. First, the pawnbroker would never give the person the full value of his property. In fact, you might only get a fraction of the actual value of the property. Secondly, the ticket had an expiration date on it. What this meant was that if you did not redeem your property before the ticket expired, you would lose your ownership rights to the property. The pawnbroker could now sell the item to whomever he wanted at a substantially higher price than was originally negotiated.

Have you, during desperate times, pawned away your faith in God? Maybe you pawned away your health in exchange for some cheap pleasure. Have you pawned away your integrity in order to make a quick dollar? Did you pawn away your family just to satisfy your own selfish desires? Too many of God's people have put their visions, dreams, goals, families, and ministries in the pawn shop of life! For many of you the expiration date is rapidly approaching. Don't give up and "throw in the towel" just yet! The Good Shepherd is calling your name! It is time for *you* to get out of the turmoil and go to your Shepherd. *It is restoration time!*

Imagine having all those years that you wasted restored to you. What if you could buy back (redeem) some of those missed opportunities of your past? The great *I am* said He would restore your wasted years. The Good Shepherd (the Lord Jesus) has paid the price of your ticket and has redeemed your valuables! *Get up! Get your stuff! And get out of the pawn shop!* Your family needs you. Your church needs you. Your community needs you. Let this be your year of *jubilee!*

The Year of Jubilee

Let me explain. The Old Testament speaks of a certain feast that the children of Israel acknowledged and practiced based on their law. The year of jubilee was the 50th year on their calendar. This 50th year followed a cycle of seven times seven years, or 49 years. The people had been instructed to sow (plow) their fields for six years at a time.

However, in the seventh year the land was allowed to rest and was not to be plowed. This process would allow the land to be restored and to replenish vital nutrients for the next cycle.

In addition to the practical benefits of allowing the land to replenish itself, this process also taught the people valuable lessons in the restoration of their families and nation. When families fell on hard times, they were forced to sell away (pawn) some or all of their possessions to other men in the nation. In exchange, they would get enough to sustain the family. If their fortunes changed, they could go back to the person they sold their possessions to and *redeem* their property. However, if their fortunes never did improve, their property remained in the possession of the purchaser (pawnbroker) *until the year of jubilee!* When the 50th year arrived, *all* land and possessions were returned to their original owner! This way, the nation would always stay at peace among themselves, and families would be able to pass their inheritances down from one generation to another. This holiday was accompanied by celebrations and a feast throughout all the land.

> *And ye shall hallow* [make holy] *the fiftieth year, and* **proclaim liberty** *throughout all the land unto all the inhabitants thereof: it shall be a jubile unto you;* ***and ye shall return every man unto his possession, and ye shall return every man unto his family*** (Leviticus 25:10).

What an awesome passage of Scripture! The year of jubilee signified a time of liberty and restoration. If you, for whatever reason, had lost your land and possessions, this was the time when you were able to return to your land and reclaim your property.

Many of you have lost so much in these troubled times. Your personal loss may seem too great to overcome. Devastation and despair have taken over. Your situation may be the result of circumstances beyond your control, or you may have brought them on yourself. The solution to the problem is the same in either case. The Good Shepherd is here to redeem you. You need to get off the treadmill of stress, confusion, worry, strife, and anxiety. Indulge in a time of refreshing, rest, recovery, and renewal with the Bishop and Shepherd of your soul. Right now, take time in prayer to allow the Lord to restore your soul. The prophet Jeremiah spoke of a time when God's people were hurting, confused, and had no peace.

> *The harvest is past, the summer is ended, and we are not saved. For the hurt of the daughter of my people am I hurt; I am black* [in mourning or grieving]; *astonishment hath taken hold on me.* ***Is there no balm in Gilead; is there no physician there?*** *why then is not the health of the daughter of my people recovered?* (Jeremiah 8:20-22)

The people acknowledged that the summer had passed but they were not saved. They questioned whether there was a balm in Gilead. They wondered why there was no physician to help them recover their health. The Balm of Gilead was a small African or Asian tree with aromatic leaves. The leaves were used to create a salve or healing ointment that soothed and brought healing to a wound.

Today in America and all over the earth the same cry can be heard: *"Is there no balm in Gilead; is there no physician there?"* The cry is coming from the poor and destitute as well as from the rich and famous. It is a cry for healing and restoration. Can our land be healed? Can the problems of hatred, poverty, unemployment, health care, terrorism, disease, and war be resolved? With all our twenty-first century innovations and technology, the question is being asked more than ever. *Is there no balm in Gilead?*

The answer is a resounding ***yes!*** There is a balm in Gilead. What we are looking for can be found in our Good Shepherd, the Lord Jesus Christ. The apostle Peter tells us where the source of our restoration can be found. In First Peter 2, the apostle reminds us that all of us like sheep have gone astray and that Jesus, as the Lamb of God, took our place on the Cross so that we could have life and receive God's restoration. We receive this restoration when we return to the Lord, who is the Shepherd and Bishop of our souls (see 1 Peter 2:24-25). When you find yourself being overwhelmed by the daily cares of life, whisper the words of this song to yourself:

> There is a balm in Gilead
> To make the wounded whole.

There is a balm in Gilead
To heal the sin-sick soul.
Sometimes I feel discouraged,
And I think my work's in vain,
But then the Holy Spirit
Revives my soul again.
He revives my soul again.[3]

Stop everything you are doing *now*. Take the time to pray and let the Lord, who is your Good Shepherd, restore your soul.

Dear Lord, I look to You as my source of healing and restoration. In the midst of the trouble and confusion all around me, I lift my voice to You. I declare aloud that You are the lifter up of my head and the restorer of my soul. Amen

Endnotes

1. *Webster's Ninth New Collegiate Dictionary* (Springfield, MA: Merriam-Webster, 1991), s.v. "Restore."

2. W.E. Vine, *The Expanded Vine's Expository Dictionary of New Testament Words* (Grand Rapids, MI: Bethany House, 1984), s.v. "Soul."

3. "There Is a Balm in Gilead," Wikipedia, the Free Encyclopedia, September 23, 2010, Traditional Lyrics, accessed February 19, 2011, http://en.wikipedia.org/wiki/ThereIs_a_Balm_in_Gilead.

Chapter 5

He Leads Me Down the Right Path

(Jehovah-Tsidkenu) The Lord My Righteousness

In the previous chapter we talked about the common sheepfold where several shepherds kept their flocks together during the night. On some occasions, while the sheep were resting, the shepherd would go and search out the land. That way, he would know exactly where to lead the sheep later. Remember the main responsibilities of the shepherd are to feed, lead, and protect the sheep. A good shepherd knows that his reputation in the village is on the line as a herdsman. This is why the shepherd would put his own life in jeopardy to protect the flock. Jesus stated that the false shepherd does not accept this responsibility and will leave the sheep to fend for themselves.

The Good Shepherd will *never* leave the sheep at the mercy of predators! I have learned through my life's experiences that He will *cause* me to *stand and be successful* no matter what the circumstances are. This is true even when we don't always follow God's directions. In fact, God will cause you to be successful sometimes *in spite* of yourself! Remember, the nature of sheep is to go astray.

> *All we like sheep have gone astray; we have turned every one to his own way; and the Lord hath laid on Him the iniquity of us all* (Isaiah 53:6).

The Lord knows His children, and He is aware of each of our weaknesses and tendencies. This is why having a good relationship with your Good Shepherd is vital to your well-being and success. You should know that your success in this life is as important to God as it is to you. Why? Because from the *moment* you accepted the lordship of Jesus Christ in your heart and put your trust in God, *His name, His word, and His power (authority) were on the line!* (I pray that God will give you ears to hear what the Holy Spirit will reveal to you right now.)

God's Purpose and Plan

Each of us has *two* creative purposes to fulfill in our lives. One purpose is *beyond* the heavens and is eternal. The other purpose is *under* the heavens and has a specific time to be fulfilled. The first purpose is spiritual in nature, and it is the *same* for everyone. This purpose was established by God before He laid the foundations of the heavens and the earth! It was a mystery, kept in the heart of God until He revealed it unto us through the apostle Paul.

> *Having made known unto us the mystery of His will, according to His good pleasure which He hath purposed in Himself: that in the dispensation of the fulness of times He might gather together in one all things in Christ, both which are in heaven, and which are on earth; even in Him: in whom also we have obtained an inheritance, being predestinated according to the purpose of Him who worketh all things after the counsel of His own will* (Ephesians 1:9-11).

God planned for us to share in the glory and splendor of His creation throughout all eternity. Even though man fell short of God's glory, we didn't stop the plan and purpose of God for our lives. In fact, man's fall from grace and his subsequent redemption and restoration to God's grace had already been dealt with by God before He created the heavens and the earth. God knew you *before* you were born! He had already made provisions for your life here on earth *and* for all eternity! Think of that! *You* were in the heart of God before He created the heavens and earth! This means you are not here by accident or a mistake.

One of the age-old questions man has asked himself is: *Why am I here?* The answer is simple but profound.

You were created *by God* to have fellowship with Him throughout eternity!

In short, God created man to share His glory, His power, and His creation with Him forever.

> *And God said, Let Us make man in Our image, after Our likeness: and* ***let them have dominion*** *over the fish of the sea, and over the fowl of the air, and over the cattle, and over all the earth, and over every creeping thing that creepeth upon the earth* (Genesis 1:26).

Notice, God said let *them* have dominion. The text is referring to the male and the female. When God create *man* (the species), He included the man and the woman from the beginning. Both were created in His image and both were to share in His glory, power, and dominion forever! Unfortunately, man fell out of favor with God through disobedience and sin. As a result, he lost the image of God and subsequently forfeited his right to have dominion over all the works of God's hand on earth.

The good news is that man's fall *did not* change God's plan. *God's original creative purpose is His eternal creative purpose.* This means God never gave up on His creation! And God will *never* give up on you!

So God's eternal creative purpose for you, beyond the heavens, is that you are *restored* and *conformed* to the image of Jesus Christ. Consider this powerful text from the Book of Romans.

> *And we know that* ***all*** *things work together for good to them that love God, to them who are the called according to His purpose. For whom He did foreknow, He also did* ***predestinate*** *to be conformed to the* ***image*** *of His Son, that He might be the firstborn among many brethren* (Romans 8:28-29).

Do you believe that there is a divine hand in your life? For those who love God and are called according to His purpose, *all* things in your life are being worked out by God. His purpose, that you and I will be conformed to the image of Christ, was in His heart from the beginning! God does *not* make anyone receive Him or reject Him. However, God knew those who *would* hear the Gospel message and accept His gift of redemption through Jesus Christ. For those who would receive Him, God planned (predestinated) a course for your life that will bring you to your original creative purpose. Take a moment to meditate on that one for awhile. In fact, before you had even heard of the Lord, God was watching over you and protecting you from harm and danger. Some of you wouldn't even be here today but for the grace of God that kept you from seen *and* unseen dangers!

It's Not Your Time Yet

I can remember two distinct occasions when I should have died, but God intervened and spared my life. The first occurred when I was eight years old. At the time, my family was living in a tenement housing development known as the Latrobe Homes. I lived with my mother, brother, and five sisters. This development consisted of rows of "courts" that were grouped together around a small playground. Inside each court was an open area with a section called "the clothes hanger." There were poles on either side of the clothes hanger. After the mothers would wash the families' clothes, they would string a rope across the two poles and hang the clothes on the ropes. At times, especially during the summer, there would be as many as 30 clotheslines hanging across the poles. When the clothes were dry, they were taken off the lines, folded up, and taken in the house. However, the lines were usually left in place for the next time. After holding the wet clothes a number of times, the lines would begin to sag in the middle.

On one particular fall evening as the sun was setting, I was playing football with some of my friends in our court. My friend Jimmy (who always got to play quarterback) threw the ball as far as he could in my direction. I took off as fast as I could towards the clothes hanger. I *never* saw the sagging clothesline. I was running at full speed when the rope caught my neck just under the chin. I can remember coming to an abrupt stop and dangling from the rope for what seemed like an eternity. I could vaguely hear the faint cries of my friends telling me to stop goofing off. I realized later that they had no idea what was happening to me. As I hung there, with my feet curled up behind me about a foot off the ground, the rope began to cut off my air supply. I'm not sure how long I was there, but I know I began to pass out and felt completely helpless to do anything about it.

I had never been close to death (that I was aware of), but I had a strange feeling that I was going to die. Then a wonderful, miraculous thing occurred. Out of the corner of my eye, I could vaguely make out what appeared to be a very large man perched on top of the pole with one hand on the rope and the other hand holding the pole. His whole body was bright as the sun and he had a peaceful, compassionate look on his face. He looked at me and with a strong, confident voice said, *"It's not your time, son."* With that, he snapped the rope and I immediately fell to the ground, landing on my knees! I stayed there, on my knees, for several minutes shaking uncontrollably.

It was years later before I had a clear understanding of what had happened, but at the time I remember having a sense that something miraculous had taken place. I also never talked about this incident for nearly 30years for fear that people would ridicule me.

The second incident occurred when I was 12 years old. It was during the summer when all of the city's neighborhood pools are open to the public. I had gone to the pool to have some fun with several of my cousins. It was early in the afternoon on a beautiful, clear day. I have to mention that my three cousins were expert swimmers. In fact, one of them had won a number of swimming tournaments and worked part-time as a lifeguard. I, on the other hand, couldn't swim from one end of the bathtub to the other! They decided to go to the deep end (ten feet) of the pool, and dive off of the high diving board. Being the foolish young man that I was, I followed right along, not willing to let my cousins show me up. When my turn came to dive, I confidently strutted up the ladder (I was actually scared to death) and stepped to the edge of the platform.

After watching my cousins perform these beautiful dives, I figured it couldn't be that hard, right? Wrong! I have no idea what I did, but I'm told I made the biggest splash they had ever seen. I do remember about half way down thinking to myself, *You must be out of your mind.* I entered the water with a thud and sank quickly, with my back hitting the bottom of the pool. The impact knocked my mouth open and I began swallowing a lot of water. My cousins were so busy laughing that they didn't realize I was in trouble. Apparently the lifeguard on duty was busy too, since he did not jump in to save me. Again, I felt myself losing consciousness as I lay helpless at the bottom of the pool. Just as I was slipping away, I felt two strong hands take hold under my arms and start to lift me slowly up. As I ascended, a voice whispered in my ear, *"It's still not your time yet."* I was told by my cousins that I came out of the water as if I had been shot out of a rocket! They confirmed that no one had jumped in and pulled me out of the water.

I understand now that God was protecting me, even though at the time I didn't know who He was. God had a *purpose* for my life, and He has watched over me in order to bring me to that goal. God has a purpose for you also, and He has been watching over you to bring you to your goal. There have probably been times in all of our lives when God has miraculously intervened and kept you from certain destruction. You are still here in spite of all the things that have come your way. Our lives may have taken different paths, but the Lord will cause each of us to fulfill our eternal creative purpose: *To be conformed to the image of Christ.*

> *Moreover whom He did predestinate, them He also called: and whom He called, them He also justified: and whom He justified, them He also glorified* (Romans 8:30).

Each of our lives has been mapped out with different challenges and lessons. The Good Shepherd knows you personally and will move people in and out of your life to help you fulfill your creative purpose. Also, you will be placed in a variety of circumstances and situations that will test your resolve. Each of these challenges is designed to prepare you for the next level God wants to take you to. Remember, God will never put more on you than what you can bear. Unfortunately, what God *knows* I can bear and what I *think* I can bear are usually two different things!

Purpose in This Life

I mentioned earlier in this chapter that each of us has two creative purposes. We just explained the eternal purpose God has for us *beyond* the heavens—to be conformed to the image of Christ. This purpose supersedes natural boundaries and is eternal in the heavens. It is also God's original purpose for man and it is the same for everyone.

On the other hand, our second creative purpose is different for each person and has a *specific time to be fulfilled.* You might be called to be a pastor while someone else is called to be a physician. You might be a schoolteacher or a shop owner. There are evangelists and builders. You could be a CEO of a major corporation or a youth worker at a local church.

The important thing to remember is that God is also working in your life to fulfill this calling as well. There is one major difference in your two callings. Your primary creative purpose is spiritual in nature and will be experienced for all eternity, your second creative purpose (your calling) will be fulfilled here on earth and has a set time to be completed.

> *To every thing there is a season, and a* ***time to every purpose under the heaven*** (Ecclesiastes 3:1).

If you are a pastor, you have a certain amount of time to fulfill that calling. It is the same for any other purpose you may have. Put another way, you *don't* have forever to do what God wants you to do in this lifetime. There are many people who spend their entire lives doing everything except what God has for them to do. There is a reason why 80 percent of people say they are unhappy with their jobs. Too many of us are doing things we were never created to do. Wouldn't it be sad if you spent your whole life wanting to accomplish a particular thing but never actually fulfilled that goal?

You might say, "But Pastor Warren, I don't know what I was put here to do." If you want to know what your creative purpose under the sun is, you will have to go to the Source of your life.

> *For Thou hast possessed my reins: Thou hast covered me in* ***my mother's womb****. I will praise Thee; for I am fearfully and wonderfully made: marvelous are* ***Thy works****; and that my soul knoweth right well* (Psalm 139:13-14).

Go to your Good Shepherd and ask Him what He would have you do. Remember, He's the one who knows you and has put the gifts and desire in you that are necessary to fulfill your purpose.

It is important to remember that you cannot fulfill your creative purpose while following the crowd. The road to your success will at times be a lonely one. The crowd is not particularly interested in your success. If you want to be unique and accomplish things that only you can do (because God created you that way), you will have to separate yourself from the mediocre and the ordinary. Jesus was our example of a person completely motivated to fulfill His creative purpose under the heavens. After the birth of Christ, the Bible is virtually silent about Jesus' formative years. As custom would have it, He most likely followed in the footsteps of His earthly father, Joseph, and worked as a carpenter. However, the

Bible does give us a glimpse of just how focused Jesus was on fulfilling His creative purpose.

Three times a year, all the males in Israel were required to go to Jerusalem and appear before the Lord during the feast of unleavened bread, the feast of harvest, and the feast of ingathering (see Exod. 23:14-17). When Jesus was 12 years old, He accompanied His family to Jerusalem for the feast of unleavened bread (Passover). When the feast was over, the family headed back home, unaware that Jesus was not with them. When they realized that He was not with the group, they turned around and went back to Jerusalem to find Him. When they found Jesus, He was in the temple listening to and asking questions of the religious leaders. Those who heard Him were astonished at His understanding and insight. Mary, who had been worried about her Son, chided Jesus for not staying with the family. Jesus' response to her was simple yet powerful.

> *And He said unto them, How is it that ye sought Me? wist* [knew] *ye not that I **must** be about My Father's business?* (Luke 2:49)

As a young man, Jesus was already preparing to fulfill His creative purpose in life under the heavens. We do not hear any more about Jesus' life until He was about 30 years old. At that time, Jesus was baptized by John the Baptist and began His public ministry. For the next three and a half years, until His death and subsequent resurrection, Jesus turned the world *upside down!* Everything that had happened in His life prior to this time was all preparation for His short but powerful ministry. Jesus' creative purpose under the heavens was not long, but its impact is still affecting the world to this day.

God Doesn't Give Up

I can remember growing up and trying my best to fit in with the popular kids. I really wanted to be a part of the "in crowd." However, no matter how hard I tried I just didn't seem to fit all the way in. I could "hang" for a while, but eventually something would pull me away. That something, I believe, was the Spirit of God letting me know there were bigger and better things in store for me if I dared to step away from the crowd and follow the voice of the Good Shepherd!

If you're bold enough to do this, get ready for two things to happen. First, the crowd will eventually turn on you. They don't want you to show them up by doing the right thing. When you decide to walk in God's will for your life, you will automatically rub some people the wrong way. You won't even have to say anything to them. Your lifestyle and focus will be enough to put them on the defensive. Second, and more importantly, get ready to experience the most exciting times of your life! When you are focused and committed to achieving your goals, doors will start to open that you didn't even know existed. God will bring people into your life who will serve as resources for inspiration, instruction, and blessings.

But what happens when we take a side road and deviate from God's purpose for our life? It is safe to assume that a lot of us have taken some missteps in our lives. After all, our nature as sheep is to go astray. What happens to God's plan when we stumble and fall? *Nothing!* That's right—God's plan is still in place even when we deviate off course. God can handle our mistakes. Sometimes we get so frustrated with our own failures that we're ready to give up. However, God will not give up on you. Heaven does not go into crisis mode because you made a mistake. It's not as if your mistake caught the Lord off guard. The Good Shepherd knows us and has already made provisions for us to be successful even when we stumble.

I can remember a very low time in my life when I had strayed away from God's creative purpose for me. To put it bluntly, I had sinned against God. The consequences of my actions had taken a toll on me as well as my family. I was drained mentally, physically, and spiritually. To make matters worse, I was still pastoring a church at this time. On the surface, it appeared that everything was OK for a while. However, I knew that things weren't right in my heart. Eventually, as information about me came out, people who had known me for years began to turn away from me. I was told by a "friend" that I was a laughingstock and no longer deserved the respect of my peers. Many labeled me an outcast and predicted that I would lose everything.

I learned that one day you can be on top of the world and the next day you could be in the depths of the valley!

The fact is, nothing anyone said about me could compare to the torment I put myself through. However, I remember one cold night I had reached my breaking point. I got up about two o'clock in the morning and from my knees cried out to the Lord for His mercy. After several hours of weeping and soul searching, the Good Shepherd spoke to my heart. He assured me that I was forgiven and that He had *never* given up on me! The Spirit of the Lord then directed me to a passage of Scripture that changed my life.

> *For I will **restore** health unto thee, and I will **heal** thee of thy wounds, saith the Lord; because they called thee an **Outcast**, saying, This is Zion, whom no man seeketh after* (Jeremiah 30:17).

I have not looked back since that time! Incidentally, the Lord told me to not worry about my reputation any more. When I asked Him why not, He quietly responded, *"Because you don't have any!"*

God won't give up on you for His name's sake. The Lord has invested a lot in you already. In fact, God had to sacrifice His only begotten Son in order to fulfill His purpose in your life. He definitely isn't going to bail out on you if you stumble and fall now. Because God is on your side, it doesn't matter who or what comes against you. Because God has already invested His best in you, He will certainly see you through until you have fulfilled His purpose for your life.

Think of it this way—God has put His name and reputation on the line for your success. You must learn to trust that God is leading you in the right direction and will pick you up, if necessary, when you fall. God will mend your wounds and set you back on course again. I know many people who have made bad choices in their lives. The consequences of those bad decisions could have been devastating. However, because of God's mercy and grace they were able to recover and move forward. Instead of wallowing in shame and self-pity, they repented and asked God to cleanse them. This allowed for a quick recovery, and they were able to get on with their lives. A wonderful example of how God's mercy can help a person recover from their mistakes is found in the life of King David.

David's Sin

David, the wonderful shepherd boy and the mighty king of Israel, was also an *adulterer* and a *murderer!* Second Samuel 11 gives the account of how David, king of Israel, used his position to take advantage of a young, beautiful married woman named Bathsheba. One evening, while David was walking on the roof of the palace, he spotted Bathsheba bathing herself (her house was evidently near the palace). The Bible notes that she was beautiful to look upon. David asked his servants to find out who Bathsheba was.

Eventually, David had her brought to the palace where he promptly committed adultery with her and sent her back home. David did this even though he knew Bathsheba was the wife of Uriah, one of his chief military leaders. When word reached David that Bathsheba was pregnant, he concocted a scheme to bring Uriah home (under the guise of giving him a rest from the battle).

The plan was to have Uriah sleep with his wife and thereby cover up David's sin. Everyone, including Uriah, would assume he was the father of the child nine months later. David even got Uriah drunk hoping this would help his plan. However, Uriah being the good soldier that he was would not take pleasure with his wife while his men were out on the battlefield. David then sent orders to his captain to put Uriah on the front line and pull the rest of the men back, leaving Uriah exposed to the enemy. To add insult to injury, David sent for Bathsheba soon after she was finished mourning her husband and made her his wife. I didn't make this up, folks! Read your Bible. Hollywood doesn't have anything over the drama found in God's Word.

Under Jewish law, adultery was punishable by death (see Lev. 20:10). God sent the prophet Nathan to David to confront him with his sin. David, who could have had the man of God put to death immediately, acknowledged his sin and accepted God's judgment upon him. And although David and Bathsheba lost their first child, God blessed their union with a second child. That child was Solomon, who later inherited his father's throne and become one of the greatest rulers of all time!

Why was God so forgiving of David in spite of his shortcomings? Mainly because of the relationship David had with God. David fully appreciated the mercy of God. He understood that his standing with God was based on God's mercy and love for him and *not* on his own ability (or lack of ability) to always do the right thing. First Samuel 13:14 states that God chose David over Saul to be king over Israel because David was a man *after God's own heart.* Each of us can look back at a time in our own lives when we failed God miserably and did not deserve the mercy of God.

> *We have sinned with our fathers, we have committed iniquity, we have done wickedly. Our fathers understood not Thy wonders in Egypt; they remembered not the multitude of Thy mercies; but provoked Him at the sea, even at the Red sea. Nevertheless He saved them for* ***His name's sake****, that He might make His mighty power to be known* (Psalm 106:6-8).

Your Good Shepherd wants you to know that He has invested all that Heaven has to help you fulfill your creative purposes, here on earth and throughout eternity. In fact, God already sees you as successful and victorious! *You* must now see yourself as God sees you—righteous, victorious, successful, and an overcomer. Let me share with you another example of God's ability to change a life and fulfill His purpose in you for *His* name's sake.

Second Chances

From 1978 until 1990, I taught a Bible class at several of the prisons in my home state of Maryland. I was a volunteer worker with a wonderful Christian ministry called Teen Challenge. This organization would send ministers into prisons throughout the country who would share the Word of God with the inmates. They also had centers established outside the prisons where the young men could go once they were paroled. These centers would help the ex-offenders prepare for re-entry into society.

Every Wednesday evening I taught a class at the Maryland Correctional Institution at Jessups, or MCIJ. Each Wednesday about 50 inmates (a truly *captive* audience) would sit for two hours and listen to me teach the Word. Some of the men were doing hard time for crimes such as armed robbery and attempted murder. Many of these young men, however, were not hardened criminals but had simply made some wrong turns in their lives. Most simply needed someone to take the time and show them a better way of living. Some of the men actually attended the classes for more than three years. Over the years I had the privilege of seeing many of them come out of prison and become strong members of their communities. In fact, a number of them became active members of their local churches and several are *pastors* of active, thriving churches to this day! Let me tell you the remarkable story of one of these men.

Manuel, a young man from Puerto Rico, came into my class one Wednesday night and sat down in the front row. He listened intently to me as I taught the Word of God. At the time I did not know that he could only speak a little English. As I taught, he would flip through a Bible written in Spanish that had been given to him by another minister from Teen Challenge Ministries. After each class, Manuel would come up to me and ask as many questions as time would permit about the Bible, God, and anything else he could think of. He later told me that he had been caught smuggling drugs from Miami to New York and had left a wife and small child at home in Puerto Rico. I had never seen anyone so eager to learn about the Bible. Eventually, Manuel's English greatly improved and he became a powerful Christian man while still in prison. He taught Spanish to the other inmates and continued to grow in the Lord.

After his parole, Manuel entered one of the Teen Challenge centers in Maryland. His commitment and dedication to becoming what God had always intended for him was remarkable! He ultimately rose to become the *director* of the center! In time, he was able to bring the rest of his family here with him. Over 20 years later, he was still going strong, pastoring a church and helping other young men find their purpose in life. Manuel's mistakes led him to the brink of destruction, but *mercy* wouldn't let him drown! God was working out Manuel's creative purpose for his life even when he didn't know it.

You may have taken some crooked paths that have led you to the brink of physical, financial, emotional, and spiritual ruin. Don't give up on yourself. Even if others have given up on you, your Good Shepherd will *not* give up on you.

The Lord *will* lead you in the paths of righteousness. Even when we make bad choices and fall down, the Good Shepherd will pick us up and put us on the right path for *His* name's sake.

Chapter 6

Down in the Valley

(Jehovah-Shamma) The Lord Who Is There

Yea, though I walk through the valley of the shadow of death, I will fear no evil: for Thou art with me; Thy rod and Thy staff they comfort me (Psalm 23:4).

Over the years, this passage of Scripture has provided comfort and solace to countless grieving families during times of bereavement. We thank God that He is there with us at these difficult times. It gives us a sense of peace knowing that our loved one is safe and has gone to a better place.

What you may not have considered is that there are actual places in the Middle East, particularly in Palestine, that have long been referred to as valleys of death. I spoke to a shepherd who had on several occasions gone through some of these areas. The shepherd was constantly on the lookout for suitable pastures for the sheep to graze in. Sometimes the shepherd, along with the flock, would have to travel great distances through winding, dangerous paths. These paths would often lead through mountains that were filled with overhanging cliffs and deep ravines. At certain points, the passageway in these valleys would get so narrow that only one sheep at a time could pass through. The passage became even more treacherous when the sheep encountered deep trenches that had developed over time by nature.

These trenches or gorges were several feet deep and sometimes would leave one side higher than the other. Also, the walls of the mountains could be hundreds of feet in height and at certain points would jut out toward the other side. The natural formation of the cliffs would at times obstruct the sunlight and as evening approached often created *shadows* that would shift as the sun moved across the mountains.

Imagine the effect this would have on the sheep, which by nature were timid and easily spooked. When the shepherd came to one of the gorges, he would have to jump across to the other side first. He would then have to coax the sheep, one at a time, to jump across to him. For the sheep, which were probably already fearful of the ominous shadows that were moving about, this entire experience proved to be unnerving and stressful. At this point, some of the sheep might want to turn around and go back. However, there wasn't enough room to turn around.

Fortunately, the shepherd knew how to get the sheep to jump across to the other side. His soothing, *familiar* voice was enough for the sheep to lay aside their fears and follow the voice of their shepherd. Remember, the sheep *know* the voice of the Good Shepherd and the Good Shepherd *knows* His sheep (see John 10:4). In addition to this traumatic experience, the shepherd had to deal with an even more dangerous prospect.

The Shepherd's Rod

The shepherd carried with him at all times a rod or a staff. Sometimes he would carry both of these items with him. The rod and the staff were the basic tools of the shepherd. They were also interchangeable in their uses.

The staff was primarily used to support the shepherd. He would use it to lean on when he got tired from the constant walking and standing. It also provided support when crossing the rugged, mountainous terrain.

I fractured my ankle several years ago after slipping and falling on a wet pavement. During my rehabilitation, I had to use a cane for support until I was able to walk on my own again. I remember how exhausting it was to try and get around without the aid of my cane. I'm sure that the staff, a simple piece of wood, was nonetheless a valuable tool in the hands of the shepherd.

The rod, on the other hand, was used for two other distinct purposes. Those two purposes were for fighting and correction. The shepherd was always on the lookout for wild animals such as dogs and wolves, which would stalk the sheep as they hunted for food. These beasts of prey would sometimes hide down in the gorges, out of sight, waiting to capture an unsuspecting sheep that might fall into the pit. This became known as the "valley of death."

As the sheep attempted to jump across the gorge to the waiting shepherd, one would unfortunately lose its footing and fall into the pit. If not for the skill and quick action of the shepherd, the sheep would be easy prey for the predator. The good shepherd, who is fearless and strong, would use the rod to bang the beast on the head and continue fighting until he had warded off the danger. Then the shepherd would use the other end of the rod, which had a crook at the end, and skillfully place it under the front legs of the sheep and hoist it up to safety on the other side. The entire experience would hopefully be over quickly without the shepherd losing any of his flock.

> *I am the good shepherd: the good shepherd giveth his life for the sheep. But he that is an hireling, and not the shepherd, whose own the sheep are not, seeth the wolf coming, and leaveth the sheep, and fleeth: and the wolf catcheth them, and scattereth the sheep* (John 10:11-12).

The Rod of Correction

God uses a rod in a similar fashion when dealing with us. The Lord uses the rod to help pull us out of danger.

The rod is referred to as the "rod of correction." However, we should view God's correction as instructive and not punitive (punishing) in nature. During the course of our lives, we all stumble and fall. God can handle our missteps. The road each of us travels is littered with pitfalls. In addition, there are predators lurking about waiting to pounce on every mistake we make. Your Good Shepherd is *not* like that!

> *He hath not dealt with us after our sins; nor rewarded us according to our iniquities. For as the heaven is high above the earth, so great is His mercy toward them that fear Him. As far as the east is from the west, so far hath He removed our transgressions from us* (Psalm 103:10-12).

However, we tie the Lord's hands when we do not trust Him enough to follow His voice. Our lack of trust is indicative of our lack of relationship with the shepherd. Imagine what would happen to the sheep if they did not know and trust the voice of their shepherd during a time of crisis. In fact, the strength of the bond between the shepherd and sheep was critical to the survival of the flock, especially during times of trouble. The middle of the crisis is not the best time to find out that you don't really know your shepherd. I once heard a wise old man say, "It's not easy to build your house while in the middle of a hurricane!"

God's rod of correction today is His *Word*. He uses His Word to give instruction, guidance, comfort, and correction to His children. On the other hand, those who seek to devour God's people should beware! The Good Shepherd will use the same rod to bang them on the head and destroy them if necessary. The Lord will always protect His flock!

> *My son, despise not the chastening of the Lord; neither be weary of His correction: for whom the Lord loveth He correcteth; even as a father the son in whom he delighteth* (Proverbs 3:11-12).

I have often heard people say that when something bad happens to them they believe God is punishing them. Society tends to blame God for all the disasters that take place throughout the earth. Even the insurance companies refer to natural calamities as "acts of God." Isn't it odd that whenever something good happens to us, we stick our chest out and say, "Look at what I've done," but when something bad happens we point our finger at God and say, "Why did You do that?" The truth is, good and bad things happen to "good" people, and good and bad things happen to "bad" people. I've even heard preachers tell people that God will make your kids sick in order to punish you or teach you a lesson.

Do you *really* know your Shepherd? Do you understand that He is not out to destroy you but to feed and lead you and protect you *from* the destroyer? If we believe that God is out to get us every time we stumble and fall, how will we have faith in Him to deliver us? If I believe that God would give my child a disease because He was angry at me for doing something wrong, why would

I then ask Him to touch my child and make him better? God is *Jehovah Rophe—the Lord thy Healer!*

It is imperative that you understand the Lord will move Heaven and earth to *save* you not *destroy* you.

> *The thief cometh not, but for to steal, and to kill, and to destroy: I am come that they* [the sheep] *might have life, and that they might have it more abundantly* (John 10:10).

Through the Valley

Jesus, while giving the Sermon on the Mount, taught His disciples that God would not give evil gifts to His people when they asked for something good. He went further to explain that if we, being evil, knew how to give good things to our children, how much more would our heavenly Father give good things to those who ask Him (see Matt. 7:9-11)?

We look around the earth and see so much suffering and death that we grope for reasons to somehow explain it all. When people can't come up with logical explanations, they will usually just blame it on God or some mystical, unseen force. The fact is there are many different reasons and causes for the terrible things we see in life. They have been a part of the human experience for time immemorial. Some are the result of naturally occurring phenomena such as earthquakes, hurricanes, and drought. These calamities usually lead to sickness, starvation, and death. Others are the result of man's own destructive nature such as abuse, violence, and war. These behaviors also lead to pain, suffering, and death.

Instead of blaming God for all of the ills of society, we should be turning to Him for His grace and mercy. The Lord really does want to save us. He does, however, need our cooperation. God will always respect man's right to choose his own destiny. You must make the quality decision to trust the Good Shepherd when you are in the midst of your valley experience.

Do not allow fear of failure to keep you from going through your valley. Remember, the operative word is *through*. You don't stay *in* the valley. You go *through* the valley. You may even slip and fall when you go through. There will often be mistakes and shortcomings. However, not all valley experiences are caused by mistakes or sin. Sometimes there are unseen forces in operation that will attempt to pull you down and destroy you.

I remember going through a valley experience when I was 21 years old. A spirit of fear had gripped my mind, and I had convinced myself that I would be dead by the age of 25. There was nothing physically wrong with me that I was aware of, so there was no logical reason for me to feel this way. I now know that a vicious, unclean spirit of fear had attacked my mind and heart and was determined to destroy my life. At the time, I was a part of a growing, thriving church ministry. I played the drums for the church and sang on the choir. I was also attending college and on the surface appeared to have everything going my way. However, on the inside I was tormented by these thoughts of imminent disaster and death. I was too ashamed to tell anyone about what I was going through. As I sank deeper and deeper into despair, my ability and desire to do the things I normally did began to suffer. Fear has a paralyzing effect on people. If left unchecked, it will eventually consume your every thought. Fear can also have a debilitating effect on the physical body. Let me explain.

Our bodies can sense when danger is imminent and they will prepare to protect themselves. The body has two small organs located near the kidney that are called the *adrenal glands*. When the body is in a state of fear, these glands will secrete a hormone known as *epinephrine* or adrenaline. This secretion raises the blood pressure, increases the heart rate, and prepares the body to defend itself. We have all heard stories of extraordinary feats of strength being displayed by ordinary people during times of crises. However, a person who is constantly in a state of fear will continue to produce adrenaline even though there is no actual danger present. The excess secretion will spill over into the bloodstream and produce a negative effect. Instead of superhuman strength, the person will experience mental and physical fatigue. Over time, the body will eventually shut itself down. This is the state I found myself in as I approached my 25th birthday. I was truly in the *valley* of despair.

But I was *not* alone! The Good Shepherd was there all the time. He was not going to let me perish. I was praying every day and asking God to help me. Unfortunately, my faith was weak and my strength was almost gone. I may not have had enough *faith* to walk on the water like Peter, but thank God, *mercy* wouldn't let me drown! The Good Shepherd used His rod to pull me up. The Lord sent a dear saint into my life who helped me out of this condition. Without telling the person about what I was going through, she gave me a list of Scriptures and a set of cassette tapes that dealt with the subject of fear! Every day for several months I would read those Scriptures, listen to the tapes, and pray to my Good Shepherd. The Lord not only brought me out of that valley but also taught me how to trust Him no matter what my circumstances are.

Peace in the Valley

> ***What time I am afraid,*** *I will trust in Thee. In God I will praise His word, in God I have put my trust;* ***I will not fear*** *what flesh can do unto me* (Psalm 56:3-4).

These powerful words were penned by David when he was surrounded by his enemies. These enemies were attempting to destroy his life, but God would always deliver him out of their hands. David had learned to trust God while spending time watching his father's sheep. He had fought off the predators that tried to destroy the flock. We must also spend time with our Good Shepherd in order to develop the trust we will need to go through our valleys.

Valley experiences in this life are inevitable. What valley are you in? Is it a valley of despair, sickness, loneliness, betrayal, poverty, indecision, or failure? While in the valley, you may also have to deal with predators lurking about waiting to take advantage of your misfortune. Sadly, those who were able to help us in the past are now dealing with their own problems. Still others have been in the valley so long they are not sure if they will ever come out.

Remember, you are not going to stay in that valley. You are only going *through* the valley. Do *not* despair. Your Good Shepherd *will* bring you out, and you *will* get to the green pastures on the other side! Even if you have fallen down, the Good Shepherd is there to pull you up and bring you to safety. Even if there are predators waiting to devour you, the Lord will protect.

The journey to fulfilling your creative purpose and achieving your goals will send you through some narrow, winding, rocky places. At times there will be enemies surrounding you who will attempt to defeat you. This is when knowing your Shepherd will sustain you. There will be times when you will need God to move on your behalf right away. However, the answer may not always come right away. This is when time spent with the Lord will have its greatest benefit. As we wait on the Lord, we learn to trust Him.

This happened to me several years ago. I had asked God to intervene in a critical situation I was dealing with. Nothing happened for a while. So I continued to pray about the matter each day. I included thanksgiving and praise in my daily prayers. I even solicited others to pray the prayer of agreement with me. After several months had passed, the answer finally came. I was thankful that God had answered me even though it had taken a while. But I was curious about why the answer had been delayed. So I went back to God in prayer and asked Him why it took so long for the answer to come. I knew He could have moved right away. The Lord's reply was very simple: *"Because I enjoyed talking to you every day."*

The fact is, without the valley experiences in our lives some of us wouldn't ever feel the need to commune with God. God *does* hear us the moment we pray to Him. And He has already made provision for our needs long before we showed up in a state of panic and desperation. We have to learn how to *wait* on the Lord. Waiting on the Lord *does not* mean sitting around worrying and complaining about the situation. We "wait" on the Lord the same way a waiter "waits" on a table. When you go to a restaurant and sit down at the table, you expect the waiter to come and serve you. In the same manner, we should go to the Lord ready to serve Him!

Consider this—prayer, from our perspective, is when we try to get God to leave His state of *peace* and come into our state of *crisis*. We think that by getting God in a crisis mode, He will move more quickly for us. However, prayer from God's perspective is God getting us to leave our state of *crisis* and enter into His state of *peace*. There are four important facts to remember when you engage in prayer:

- The answer is never in doubt when we pray according to God's Word.
- God will never panic, and He doesn't go into crisis mode.
- The more we trust God, the shorter the wait time will seem.
- The more time we spend in prayer, the more we will trust Him.

Learn from the valley experiences in your life as well as the mountaintop experiences. Your Good Shepherd is with you during all your ups and downs, victories and setbacks. However, you will *really* come to know and appreciate the Lord as you go *through* the difficult times in your life.

May God's surpassing *peace* rule in your heart.

Chapter 7

Eatin' Good in a Bad Neighborhood

(Jehovah-Nissi) The Lord My Banner

I have stated that the three main responsibilities of the shepherd are to feed, lead, and protect the sheep. One of the daily responsibilities of the shepherd was searching for sufficient edible grass for the flock to graze on. This task was made more difficult because of the presence of poisonous plants that grew among the grass. Many of these plants that grew in the field were toxic to the digestive system of the sheep. The sheep's teeth were designed to eat grass, weeds, shrubs, and anything else growing in the field. This created a problem for the shepherd because *everything* looked good to the sheep. Once they put their heads down and started grazing, the sheep were not going to be picky about what they ate.

The shepherd was responsible for knowing which plants were edible and which plants were poisonous. The poisonous plants were *enemies* to the sheep's well-being.

And when he putteth forth his own sheep, he goeth before them, and the sheep follow him: for they know his voice (John 10:4).

A good shepherd would go ahead of the flock and search out the grazing pastures. When he found suitable fields, he would diligently go through that field and pull out all the plants that could harm the sheep if eaten. The shepherd would uproot these poisonous plants (the enemy) and leave them out in the middle of field. As the sun rose, the searing heat would scorch the plants and dry them out. The pasture is now *prepared* for the sheep to graze in later that morning. When the sheep came into the field, they were now able to eat *in the presence of their enemies! Selah.*

By preparing the field for the sheep beforehand, the shepherd would avoid some of the problems that could have afflicted the flock.

The shepherd needed to have expert knowledge of all the various plants that were indigenous to the region. In addition, he had to be diligent and watchful, ensuring the safety of the sheep. If one of the sheep wandered off or became ill, the shepherd would take the time to find the sheep, and once found he would bring it back to the flock and bind its wounds. At times, if necessary, the shepherd would have to carry the lost or injured sheep on his shoulders. In Luke 15, Jesus gave the parable of the one lost sheep. The Pharisees and scribes had been critical of Jesus because He associated with "*publicans and sinners.*" Jesus compared His association with the common people to that of the shepherd who devotes his time to the sheep that needed him most. Jesus used the parable to show that a good shepherd would not allow even *one* sheep to be lost.

Feed the Flock

The role of the leaders in the church is very similar to that of the shepherd. The pastor's role in particular is most closely aligned to that of a shepherd. The word *pastor*, as used in the Old and New Testaments, literally means "shepherd" or "one who tends a flock." In fact, the members of a local church are often referred to as the "flock."

The pastors have a unique relationship with the people of God. They will spend more time with the flock than any of the other ministers. The pastor is usually the official at all important milestones during a person's life. Birth, baptism, christening, marriage, ordination, and death are examples of these milestones. Also, the pastor's responsibilities include providing counseling and visiting the sick. However, the *main* responsibility of the pastor/shepherd is to *feed* the sheep.

> *Feed the flock of God which is among you, taking the oversight thereof, not by constraint, but willingly; not for filthy lucre, but of a ready mind; neither as being lords over God's heritage, but being examples to the flock* (1 Peter 5:2-3).

In these two verses, Peter charges the pastors to feed the sheep. He also sets forth the proper attitude pastors should have as they carry out their responsibilities. Notice, the pastor is to:

- *Feed* the flock of God
- Exercise the oversight, or supervision, of the flock
- Perform his duties *willingly* and not by constraint (force)
- Should not be in it for the money—must be incorruptible
- Must always be prepared (have a ready mind)
- Must not *usurp* authority (rule by force)
- Must set a good example for the flock.

The well-being of sheep is dependent upon the skill and knowledge of their shepherd. In a similar manner, the well-being of the church is dependent on the skill and knowledge of its pastor. A wise old pastor I knew would often say, "Like priest, like people." In other words, the state of the sheep was a reflection of the shepherd's care for them. A healthy, well-fed flock was the result of careful planning and hard work on the part of the shepherd. A healthy, well-fed congregation is also the result of careful planning and hard work on the part of the pastor.

God's will for each of you is that you are nourished and properly cared for by those He has put over you. In fact, the apostle John expressed God's *highest* will for your life:

> *Beloved, I wish* [will] *above all things that thou mayest prosper and be in health, even as thy soul prospereth* (3 John 2).

God wants His people to be healthy and prosperous. But notice that the basis for this state of wellbeing is that your *soul* is healthy and prosperous. A healthy soul is one that is in fellowship with God. In order to fellowship with God, you must pray and study His Word. In addition, there are other things you can do that will help you fulfill God's highest will for you. Qualities such as persistence, hard work, and determination are necessary to achieve God's highest will for your life. People who are successful in this life will not quit until they have achieved their goals. *You* must also refuse to quit until you have fulfilled *your* creative purpose.

Godly Instruction

There is another important factor to consider. I have had the opportunity to talk with many successful and highly motivated people. Every one of them shared a common factor that helped him achieve his goals. Each one said there was a person that took the time to teach him. This teacher, or mentor, was there to offer instruction and guidance. In some cases, even discipline was used to help correct mistakes and failures. In every case, though, the instruction and discipline was administered with care and compassion.

No one person has all the answers to every problem. However, there is always someone who has been through whatever you are experiencing and can offer guidance and encouragement when it is needed. By following the instructions of those who have been charged with your care, you can avoid many of the mistakes you might otherwise have made.

God brings certain people into our lives at various times for a reason *and* a season. He will also place a particular person in your life to watch over you throughout your seasons. This person will make sure you are "eating" the right things. This means receiving sound instruction and guidance from the Word of God and your mentor. They will steer you away from the poisonous things that can harm or even kill you. Remember the old adage, "You are what you eat"? This is absolutely true when it comes to feeding your soul (mind). The sheer amount of false and negative information being peddled in our society today is mind-boggling!

It is disturbing to see so many well-intentioned and seemingly intelligent people chase after every so-called "new revelation" that comes out today. I was approached by a gentleman who had been exposed to one of these "new revelations." One Wednesday night as I was leaving my prison class, I was approached by a fellow minister who had been conducting a Bible class in a different part of the prison. This well-meaning brother was so excited that he could hardly contain himself. As he came near to me, he yelled out, "Pastor, I've got a tape I want you to listen to that will *blow your mind!*" Although I'm not particularly interested in having my mind blown, my curiosity got the better of me. I asked him what the tape was about. His response was very interesting and not a little disturbing. He said, "I don't really understand all of it because it's *so deep*. But this is the new wave of the Holy Spirit that's going to turn the Church upside down!"

First, the Church doesn't need to be turned "upside down"; it needs to be turned upright! Second, the Holy Spirit doesn't *ride* new waves of revelation. The truth of God's Word is the same throughout time and eternity. *We* simply come to understand more of the Word through study and application. However, God's truth is constant and unchanging. Remember, no matter what new math comes out, two plus two will always equal four!

After listening to about five minutes of the tape, I had to turn it off. The speaker was completely lost, and it was impossible to follow the message. The next time I saw the minister I returned his tape and cautioned him to be careful of the things he listened to. He told me that I just wasn't "deep enough" to handle this new revelation.

Most of us are careful about what we put into our bodies. You should be even more careful about what you feed your mind. You must guard your heart from all the negativity and misinformation being broadcast today. This includes bad information from the secular world as well as the church world.

Keep thy heart with all diligence; for out of it are the issues of life (Proverbs 4:23).

Every day a new product comes out that promises to solve all of life's problems. For example, the diet industry does billions of dollars in business annually because they claim to be able to get rid of unwanted fat easily. People will pay any amount for a pill that promises to help them lose weight without any effort. Television is replete with infomercials that promise to do everything from making you younger to curing all your illnesses. In reality, the complex challenges of today cannot be solved by well-intentioned politicians or fast-talking pitchmen on your television. It is not surprising that we live in a cynical and confused society that harbors a deep mistrust of all who are in authority. Even preachers have taken to giving the flock exactly what they want instead of feeding them the Word of God.

Don't Cut No Corners!

The apostle Paul had some strong advice for one of his disciples named Timothy. Timothy was raised in a Christian home by his mother Eunice and his grandmother Lois (see 2 Tim. 1:5). He was mentored by Paul and became the pastor of the church at Ephesus at a young age. Ephesus was a thriving metropolis in Asia Minor during the early years of the Church. It was an important cultural and religious center at that time. Ephesus was also steeped in pagan traditions and false doctrine. Timothy was responsible for teaching the church and guiding it in the right direction.

Apparently, young pastor Timothy was having a difficult time keeping the faithful from being influenced by all the false teachings. The aged and experienced apostle Paul wrote two epistles to Timothy during this difficult time in his life. In an effort to encourage Timothy to remain strong, Paul had this to say:

> *Preach the word; be instant in season, out of season: reprove, rebuke, exhort with all longsuffering and doctrine. For the time will come when* ***they will not endure sound doctrine;*** *but after their own lusts shall they heap to themselves teachers,* ***having itching ears;*** *and* ***they shall turn away their ears from the truth,*** *and shall be turned unto fables* (2 Timothy 4:2-4).

We are living in the time that Paul predicted would come. Too many people do not want to hear the truth. Religious leaders as well as politicians have found greater success when they tell the people what they want to hear. It seems the more foolish the message and outlandish the messenger, the more some people will gravitate toward it. Some time ago I heard that on any given day, there are at least 35 people in America (most are in California) who claim to be Jesus Christ. The amazing part is that *all* of them have a group of people who follow them!

Years ago, when I had just started out in ministry, I received some good advice from an unlikely source. I was in my early 20s and had been invited to come and speak at a little church in the small town of Vienna, Maryland. When I arrived in town, there were about 30 parishioners packed into this tiny, brick building on a hot Sunday morning. After standing and singing for about *two* hours (with no air conditioning), they sat down and eagerly waited for me to preach the Word. I was about ten minutes into my sermon when a young man sitting in the back of the church yelled out, *"Don't cut no corners, preacher!"* Every so often as I continued to preach, he would yell out the same phrase. Each time he said this, the rest of the congregation would yell, *"Amen!"* I can tell you this—I have never preached so hard in my life! Obviously, the young man was encouraging me to give it to him straight and not "pull any punches." Thirty years later, I still remind myself of that good advice whenever I stand in front of an audience to speak.

Today more than ever, you need a true shepherd who will give it to you straight and not *cut any corners*. In the construction business, this concept is vitally important. You would not knowingly hire a builder or repairman who had a reputation for doing *shoddy* work. When a builder uses inferior materials and inexperienced workers, he is *cutting corners*. This practice can lead to greater expenses later and in some cases injury or even death.

When our religious and political leaders decide to cut corners, it can lead to similar consequences. The apostle Paul addressed this concern with the religious leaders of his day.

> *Take heed therefore unto yourselves, and to all the flock, over the which the Holy Ghost hath made you overseers, to* ***feed the church of God,***

which He hath purchased with His own blood. For I know this, that after my departing shall grievous wolves enter in among you, ***not sparing the flock*** (Acts 20:28-29).

Stay Strong

Today more than ever, you need a true shepherd who will lead you in the right direction, feed you good food, and protect you from the predators in our society. A short time ago I encountered a Christian woman, whose church I had preached at, in a local food market. She was excited to see me and invited me to come back to her church. Her church congregation had recently installed a new pastor. The woman said I *had* to come to the church because this new guy was a "show-stopper"! Call me old-fashioned, but if I wanted to see a "show-stopper" I'd go to the theater.

I go to church to hear the Word of God and to fellowship with like-minded believers. Unfortunately, while the church tries to compete with Hollywood by putting on its own sideshow, too many people leave church on Sunday morning without receiving the spiritual nourishment they needed. If the shepherds don't give the flock what they need, the sheep will wander off and feed on anything they can find.

Here are some practical steps you should take that will help you and your families stay strong during these difficult times.

In all decisions, great and small, take the time to fellowship with God. Praise Him for all the things He has already done in your life. While in prayer, ask your Good Shepherd to lead and guide you each day. Remember, God is not off in some corner of the universe, unaware of you and your circumstances. He *is not* an absentee dad! The Lord is right here, right now, ready to lead you every step of the way. You may have already lost your job, your house, your health, your family, and even your faith. *But you haven't lost God!* More importantly, *God hasn't lost you!* Take a moment to acknowledge His presence in your life right now.

> *Thy word is a lamp unto my feet, and a light unto my path* (Psalm 119:105).

You must have a shepherd (pastor, teacher, mentor) in your life. This person will feed you God's Word, lead you in the right direction for your life, and protect you from those things that would destroy you. A good shepherd will never drive you like cattle but will lead by example and protect you from all that would bring harm. If he is a true shepherd, he will do this because he loves you and genuinely desires to see you fulfill your creative purpose. If you do not have such a leader, ask God to direct you to the right person for you. When you have a true shepherd, be sure to submit to his or her guidance and instructions.

> *Obey them that have the rule over you, and submit yourselves: for they watch for your souls, as they that must give account, that they*

> *may do it with* ***joy****, and not with* ***grief****: for that is unprofitable for you* (Hebrews 13:17).

You are what you eat. This time-tested adage has never been truer than it is today. Another wise mentor of mine gave me some good advice years ago. He told me to listen and read with a careful heart, and to always remember to "eat the fish but throw away the bone." Your inner man, consisting of your soul and spirit, is the temple of God. It allows you to commune with Him. It is also where your personality, conscience, intellect, will, and emotions reside. Do not defile your temple by filling it with junk food. How physically healthy do you suppose you would be if your daily diet consisted of ice cream, candy, cake, and soda for breakfast, lunch, and dinner? Eventually you would become weak and lose your ability to resist disease. You would not do this to your physical body. Do not do this to your inner man. Don't let someone else dump their trash into you! Turn off the television. Put down the daily news. Purpose in your heart to spend that time with your Good Shepherd. The Lord will nourish you through His Word.

> *And I will set up shepherds over them which shall feed them: and they shall fear no more, nor be dismayed, neither shall they be lacking, saith the Lord* (Jeremiah 23:4).

Your Good Shepherd knows where the green pastures are. If you are willing to receive what He has for you, He will bless you and nourish you. You will eat good, *even in the presence of your enemies!*

Chapter 8

A Cruse of Fresh Oil

"Thou anointest my head with oil."

At the end of a busy day, the shepherd would lead the flock back to the sheepfold and secure the sheep for the night. The journey had been long and most likely compounded by a searing heat, rugged terrain, and the threat of predators. The sheep had been well fed and protected from any and all dangers. However, most of the sheep had probably sustained some minor cuts and scratches along the way. Insects and other parasites might have attached themselves to the sheep's wool or even into their eyes and ears. In addition, thorns and briers could have become lodged in the hoof. A few sheep may have sustained more substantial injuries, such as a deep cut or a fractured limb.

The shepherd would carry a measure of olive oil with him during the day and also would keep a container of oil at the sheepfold. For those sheep that may have sustained a cut or bruise to its face or other part of its body, the shepherd would call the sheep to him and personally administer the oil to the wounded area of the sheep. This "anointing" with oil was not only soothing but therapeutic to the sheep.

> *But my horn shalt Thou exalt like the horn of an unicorn: I shall be anointed with fresh oil* (Psalm 92:10).

Healing Oil

Olive oil has been used by Middle Eastern peoples for thousands of years. The oil has hundreds of common uses, including food preparation and industrial, cosmetic, and medicinal purposes. In addition, olive oil was used to anoint the skin in order to give it a healthy glow. The shepherd would use the oil to soothe the wounds of the sheep. Each sheep would go through a thorough examination by the shepherd to detect any bruises and cuts sustained during the day. If any were detected, the shepherd would anoint the affected area and carefully bind up the wound. The sheep would then have time to rest and heal before the next day's journey.

Like the sheep, many of us are not just tired and weary from the journey but are bruised and wounded. We need to have our wounds treated before we can really be at peace and rest. Have you noticed how unhappy a lot of people are with their lives? In fact, our society seems to be suffering from at best a collective state of dissatisfaction and at worst a constant state of anger and mean-spiritedness. Too many people are going into a rage at the slightest provocation. This anger and rage are the result of years of disappointments, depression, despair, unhappiness, and unresolved physical and emotional abuse. The cumulative effect from these lifetime afflictions has left multitudes of wounded and bruised people in desperate need of healing. After a long and trying day, I will often ask the Lord to anoint me with His fresh oil.

> *Is any sick among you? let him call for the elders of the church; and let them pray over him, anointing him with oil in the name of the Lord: and the prayer of faith shall save the sick, and the Lord shall raise him up; and if he have committed sins, they shall be forgiven him* (James 5:14-15).

This prescription will not only heal the body but also lift the heaviness of guilt and shame from your soul and spirit.

Jesus gives a beautiful illustration of the purpose and power of administering healing oil to a wounded person. In Luke 10, Jesus relates the story of the Good Samaritan who came to the aid of a man who had fallen upon hard times. A gentleman, probably on a business trip, was traveling from Jerusalem on his way to Jericho. Unfortunately, there were some thieves waiting to ambush him along the way. The robbers stripped him of his clothes, wounded him, and left him for dead. Bruised, naked, and near death, the man lay on the side of the road, unable to help himself. Several people, including a priest and a Levite (minister), passed by and saw the wounded man on the road but offered no assistance. Finally, a Samaritan man, who was on a journey, saw the wounded man and stopped to assist him.

The significance of the three people who came upon the wounded man should not be overlooked. Jesus mentioned that a priest and a Levite passed by (see Luke 10:31-32). You would think that these two men, given their office and work, would have certainly assisted a fellow human being in this condition. However, neither of them bothered to even stop. The Samaritans, on the other hand, were usually looked down upon and despised by the more sophisticated people of Jerusalem. Yet it was the Samaritan who stopped and had compassion on the wounded man. Notice the concern and care that was given by the Samaritan:

> *But a certain Samaritan, as he journeyed, came where he was: and when he saw him, he had* ***compassion*** *on him,* ***and*** *went to him, and bound up his wounds,* ***pouring in oil*** *and wine,* ***and*** *set him on his own beast, and brought him to an inn,* ***and*** *took care of him* (Luke 10:33-34).

The Good Samaritan poured the soothing oil on the wound to help the healing process and then bound up the wound. But the care did not stop there. After ministering to the man at the site, he then put him on his animal, carried him to an inn, and paid for a room so the man could continue to rest and recuperate! This is exactly the kind of personal care the Good Shepherd wants to provide for *you*.

The Lord Is Your Gatekeeper

There are countless numbers of people who are wounded and bruised today. Some of the wounds are visible and physical. However, many are carrying scars and bruises that may not be seen on the outside. Over time, life has seemingly sapped the energy and creativity from many. Some are carrying the scars of guilt and shame because of past sins and failures. Nothing seems to have worked out the way they planned it years ago. Others have been deceived and lied to by those they *should* have been able to trust. What becomes of all the children who are neglected, abused, and forsaken? They very often grow up and do the same thing to their children. The vicious cycle unfortunately repeats itself over and over again. As a result, many have been beaten and robbed and left for dead.

I recently was engaged in an interesting conversation with some colleagues of mine. We were asking each other who we thought were the *least* trusted people in our society today. The list we came up with was astonishing but not surprising.

1. Politicians (particularly those in high office)
2. Priests and preachers
3. Lawyers

4. Bankers and brokers
5. Journalists and other media types
6. "Experts" (so called, of any type)

Think about this list for a moment. The people listed here are the *gatekeepers* of our society! Apart from the family, these are the ones we should be able to rely upon during times of crisis. But like the priest and the Levite above, the gatekeepers have left too many bruised and battered on the side of the road. This has led to the dearth of confidence and trust in our leaders today.

However, the situation is not all bad. You may have been bruised and wounded and even left for dead by others. You may be down, but you are *definitely* not out! Through all the turmoil and trouble you may be experiencing right now, the Good Shepherd stands ready to anoint you with His healing, soothing oil of gladness! Each of us needs to step back from the clutter and clamor of the crowd and take a *big* dose of the Lord's healing oil!

When I was a little boy, my mother would use this one particular tonic for just about everything. Whenever my brother or one of my sisters would get a cold or complain of a stomachache, Mom would send one of us to the pharmacist to get a bottle of cod liver oil with wild cherry. The cod liver oil had a *horrible* taste, and after taking a spoonful the taste would linger in your mouth for days. The wild cherry flavor was added to the oil to make it taste better. (It didn't work.) However, it was the oil that was good for your system. I remember asking my mother what was the purpose of giving us the cod liver oil. Mom's reply was that everyone needed a good cleaning out every now and then! It's time for you to come to the Good Shepherd and take your medicine.

> *Thou lovest righteousness, and hatest wickedness: therefore God, thy God, hath anointed thee with the oil of gladness above thy fellows* (Psalm 45:7).

Like the Good Samaritan, the Lord will not only bind up your wounds but put you in a place where you can rest and recuperate. It doesn't matter if you are the housekeeping maid at the hotel or the president of the United States. You may be the pizza delivery man or the CEO of a major corporation. You could even be the warden of the prison or the prisoner in the cell. It doesn't matter to God.

The Good Shepherd is right there with you now. Take a moment in prayer and let Him anoint you with His fresh oil. Remember, Jesus said to come to Him if you have labored and are burdened with too many cares. He promised to give you *rest!*

CHAPTER 9

A Cup of Refreshing Water

"MY CUP RUNNETH OVER."

A typical Bedouin sheepfold would usually have a large container of water or a cistern from which water could be drawn. The water would be used to refresh and cool down the sheep. The sheep very often would be physically drained from the constant movement and the heat. Water would revitalize the body by replenishing the vitamins and nutrients lost during the journey. Each sheep would come up to the reservoir of water and satisfy its thirst. Imagine how refreshing this would be to the sheep after a long, hot day on the Palestinian countryside!

Have you ever been working outside on a very hot day? The heat will not only drain you of your strength, but it can also cause you to become dehydrated. In severe cases, dehydration can lead to fainting, disorientation, systems breakdown, or even death. Each year, over

100 people die from heat-related conditions in America alone.[1] Water is the only thing that satisfies when you are truly thirsty. In fact, a normal, healthy person can go much longer without food than without water. Fortunately, our Good Shepherd has living water that not only refreshes the body but more importantly refreshes the soul.

Living Water

In the Gospel of John chapter 4, Jesus had left Judea and was returning to Galilee. To get to Galilee, He needed to pass through the region of Samaria. While passing through Samaria, Jesus stopped at a well known as Jacob's well, located on a parcel of land near the city of Sychar (see John 4:5-6). Jesus sat down at the well at noon, exhausted from the heat of the day. Around the same time, a Samaritan woman came to the well to draw some water. The woman could not draw water in the morning with the other women from town because of her unsavory reputation as a harlot. Jesus surprised the woman by asking her to give Him a drink of water. She reminds Jesus that the Jews had no dealings with the Samaritans. Jesus' reply to the woman was direct and powerful.

> *Jesus answered and said unto her, If thou knewest the gift of God, and who it is that saith to thee, Give Me to drink; thou wouldest have asked of Him, and He would have given thee* ***living water*** (John 4:10).

It is a fact that the human body can go longer without food than it can without water. My nutritionist told me I should drink close to a hundred ounces of water a day. (I wondered if she had lost her mind!) Have you noticed that no matter what condition or illness you have when you stay in a hospital, they almost always hook you up to an IV in order to get fluids in your body? Water is essential to all life.

Our Good Shepherd promises to give us living water that not only refreshes the body but also the soul and the spirit. Each of us needs the refreshing water from the Good Shepherd at the end of a long day. For many, the long day has turned into a long week, a long month, and a long year. Unfortunately, for some of you it has been a long *life*. Along the way, you have endured oppressive heat, trials and tribulations, disappointment and disillusionment, frustrations and failures, sicknesses and setbacks. In spite of all that and more, you're *still* here and *still standing!* But you need to come to the Lord and immerse yourself in His living water. Go ahead and stick your whole face into God's refreshing water!

> *Behold, God is my salvation; I will trust, and not be afraid: for the Lord Jehovah is my strength and my song; He also is become my salvation. Therefore with* **joy** *shall ye draw water out of the wells of salvation* (Isaiah 12:2-3).

When was the last time you came to your Good Shepherd and let Him refresh you with His living water?

You have tried all of the cheap substitutes life has had to offer but have not been able to quench the thirst in your soul. All the money and material things in the world can never truly satisfy you. Too many have spent their lives in the pursuit of things and power at the expense of pursuing *real* satisfaction and contentment. There is nothing inherently wrong with having things. However, the problem is when things *have you*! I have seen too many Christians who were so busy running and laboring (even for a good purpose) that they did not have time enough to stop and refresh themselves in the Lord. This can lead to emotional and physical breakdown and spiritual burnout.

In Mark 6, John the Baptist had just been beheaded by Herod the king at the request of Herodias, the king's wife. Herodias wanted John executed because he had rebuked King Herod for taking his brother's wife. The significance of John's execution cannot be overstated. First, until Jesus came on the scene, John was the most important prophet to speak to Israel in over 400 years. John's message prepared the way for the ministry of Jesus. In addition, John was Jesus' older cousin (by six months), and he was the Lord's friend (see Luke 1:36).

When John's disciples heard what had happened, they took his body and buried it in a tomb. After they were finished, they rushed to tell Jesus what had happened. You can imagine that at this time the disciples were filled with sorrow, fear, and anger. I am sure they wanted Jesus to do something dramatic. After all, John was His cousin and had baptized Him not too long ago. I am also sure that Jesus was troubled and saddened by the bad news. However, His response to the disciples was probably not what they expected.

> *And He said unto them,* **Come ye yourselves apart** *into a desert place, and rest a while: for there were many coming and going, and they had no leisure so much as to eat. And they departed into a desert place by ship privately* (Mark 6:31-32).

Jesus recognized that the disciples were caught up in the drama of the moment and needed to get away to a quiet place and be refreshed. Notice the Lord said that many people were so busy *coming* and *going* that they didn't even have enough time to sit down and eat! Are *you* one of those people who are so busy that you don't know if you are *coming* or *going*? One preacher put it this way: "Sometimes you have to 'come apart' *before* you *come apart!*"

In these troubling and trying times that we live in today, it is very easy to get caught up in the drama of each busy day and forget to come apart in a quiet place and allow the Good Shepherd to minister to us. Have you been overwhelmed by the daily grind of your life? Has some personal or public crisis drained you physically, emotionally, and spiritually?

The Elijah Syndrome

I remember being overwhelmed by a family crisis that was both personal and public. A number of years ago, while pastoring a growing inner-city church, I received an anonymous and very disturbing call from a member of the congregation. At the time, I was married and had three children, a 2-year-old son and a set of 15-year-old twins, one boy and one girl. The caller informed my wife and me that our 15-year-old daughter was secretly seeing a 22-year-old man who had recently started attending our services *and* that our daughter was pregnant!

My first reaction was one of disbelief. After all, I was a man of God. I had been preaching for years. I had raised my children the *right* way. I had helped hundreds of families get through all kinds of crises. I had trained others for ministry. Surely the Lord would not let this happen to *me*. While still in a state of disbelief, I picked my daughter up from school as usual, but on the way home I purchased a pregnancy test from the local pharmacy. I gave the pregnancy test to my wife to administer to my daughter and went outside on the back porch. I told my wife, "Do not call me unless you have *good* news." When my wife didn't call me, I knew what that meant. After confirming the news, I immediately went into a state of shock, then panic followed by anger.

How could this happen to me and my family? Why didn't I see this coming? What will the church say about this? And the most troubling question in my mind: "How could *God* let this happen to me?" That day turned out to be one of the most difficult days I had experienced. I remember being full of embarrassment as I shared this very private and personal situation with the congregation during the following Sunday service. Although most (not all) members were supportive, it took me quite a while to recover from that experience. I continued to preach and labor in the ministry even though I harbored anger and resentment in my heart toward God for a long time. In retrospect, I realize that I never took the time to *come apart* a while and let the Good Shepherd refresh me with His living water. As a result, I became ineffective in ministry and began to drift away from the Lord in my heart.

You *cannot* truly worship and serve the Lord effectively while you are secretly harboring anger and resentment in your heart toward God (or anyone else). When I finally did take the time to get quiet before God and let Him minister to me, I began to understand that serving the Lord and laboring in ministry is not a bargaining chip that we earn from God. I realized that I was angry with God because I thought I had *earned* His favor and that nothing bad should happen to me or my family. The reality is *stuff* is going to happen to everyone in this life at one time or another. The key is that we learn to come to the Lord at those times and allow Him to refresh us and sustain us until the storm passes over.

> *Come unto Me, all ye that labour and are heavy laden, and I will give you rest. Take My yoke upon you, and learn of Me; for I am meek and lowly in heart: and ye shall find rest unto your souls* (Matthew 11:28-29).

I call my experience the *Elijah* syndrome. Let me explain. In First Kings chapter 18, the prophet Elijah experienced the greatest personal triumph of his ministry. Unfortunately, this great triumph was immediately followed by the most trying time of his life. At this time in Israel's history, the nation was under the control of the wicked king Ahab and his wife Jezebel, who was more evil than the king. Jezebel had ordered the execution of the prophets of God and had replaced them with four hundred and fifty false prophets (see 1 Kings 18:19). The children of Israel had begun to turn from the Lord and follow the false prophets of Baal. In the past, this type of backsliding by Israel would bring the judgment of God upon the people. However, this time God instructed the prophet Elijah to do something bold and different. Elijah, at the direction of the Lord, brought all the nation of Israel together at the top of Mount Carmel to witness a challenge between Jezebel's false prophets and the one true God. Elijah's purpose for this test was to turn God's people back to Him.

> *And Elijah came unto all the people, and said, How long halt ye between two opinions? if the Lord be God, follow Him: but if Baal, then follow him. And the people answered him not a word* (1 Kings 18:21).

The false prophets and Elijah were each given a bullock that was to be placed on an altar to be sacrificed. However, neither side could use fire to consume their sacrifice. The test was to have the true God answer by fire. The false prophets were first to call on their god. They called all day and into the evening but to no avail. Afterward, Elijah, who had been mocking the false prophets all day, had the people set up the altar of the Lord, which had been torn down, and placed the bullock on it. To really demonstrate the power of the true God, Elijah ordered the people to drench the altar with water three times. Elijah then prayed to God, who responded by sending His fire down to consume the sacrifice as well as all the water around the altar.

When the people saw this, they fell on their faces and worshipped the true God. Elijah, seizing the moment, had all of the false prophets of Jezebel executed. By any measure, this was a great achievement for Elijah in the eyes of all Israel. However, Elijah had developed an unhealthy sense of his own importance and invincibility. Notice in verse 22 Elijah states that *he* is the *only* remaining prophet that God had left in Israel. This false assumption by Elijah ultimately led to his removal as the voice of God to the nation of Israel. Immediately after this great miracle, Elijah *should* have *come apart* from the multitude and spent time with the Lord. He was undoubtedly exhausted and drained from the challenge. This left him weak and vulnerable to the attack of the enemy.

In First Kings chapter 19, Jezebel, as soon as she heard what Elijah had done to her prophets, issued a death warrant for Elijah's head. You would think after such a great display of the power of God that Elijah would have laughed at Jezebel's threat. Instead, exhausted and tired, he fled for his life and hid in the wilderness. While there, probably angry and discouraged, Elijah prayed to God to let him just die. Elijah's complaint was twofold:

1. He is no better than those who had come before him (see 1 Kings 19:4).
2. He is the only one who is still faithful and fighting the good fight (see 1 Kings 19:10).

Have you ever been at this place in your life? Have you been tired of fighting the good fight? Have you been discouraged because it looked like all those around you had already thrown in the towel a long time ago? Were you so dismayed that you felt like you wanted to die?

First, Elijah was correct about one thing. He actually was no better (or worse) than any of those who had come before him. *God* is the source of all our power. *God* is the miracle-worker. Second, Elijah was wrong about being the only one left who was faithful to God. Notice God's response to Elijah's assertion:

> *Yet I have left Me* ***seven thousand*** *in Israel, all the knees which have not bowed unto Baal, and every mouth which hath not kissed him* (1 Kings 19:18).

As a result, Elijah's ministry was about to come to an end. Elijah's prophetic mantle would soon fall to Elisha, the young apprentice God had chosen to replace Elijah as prophet to the nation.

God will *always* have a people who are praying and lifting up a standard against the enemy. When you start thinking that you are the only one left, you are setting yourself up for a fall. I acknowledge that there is plenty around us to be discouraged about. It often seems as if righteousness has fallen in the streets and has been replaced with evil, lust, greed, and fear. However, *God is still in control!* The Good Shepherd is always near, ready to refresh and comfort you. Here are some important instructions you must follow each day in order to avoid falling into the *Elijah Syndrome:*

- After every great victory, always *come apart* from the crowd and spend some quiet time with the Lord. Acknowledge that He is the source of your strength.
- After every setback or defeat, *come apart* from the crowd and let the Good Shepherd refresh you with His living water.
- When you feel like you are fighting the battle alone, remind yourself that there are millions of faithful partners worldwide who are still fighting the good fight of faith!
- Keep your eyes on the prize. God will always reward your faithfulness.
- Remember, you are what you eat. Turn off the radio and television. Stop feeding your mind poison. The media makes a living off of *bad* news.
- Pick up your Bible and start feeding your spirit the good news from your Good Shepherd. Saturate yourself with God's presence.
- *Know* that the Good Shepherd will cause you to succeed.

Endnote

1. Morbidity and Mortality Weekly Report, Heat-Related Illnesses and Deaths, United States, Published June 30, 1995, http://www.cdc.gov/mmwr/PDF/wk/mm4425.pdf.

Chapter 10

The Lord Has Got My Back

"Surely goodness and mercy shall follow me all the days of my life."

After years of being a pastor and teaching the Word, I have concluded that the five most dangerous words I have heard from some of my parishioners were, "I've got your back, Pastor." This statement was usually followed shortly thereafter by, "The Lord is leading me to go somewhere else, Pastor." We are living in a time when faithfulness and loyalty have taken a backseat to instant self-gratification and the "what's in it for me" syndrome.

Confidence in the Lord

When David uttered the words *"surely goodness and mercy shall follow me,"* they emanated from a strong sense of assurance and trust in God. David had faithfully taken care of his father's sheep for most of his adolescent life. I'm sure he remembered all those days and nights he had to lead the sheep from one grazing field to another. He no doubt could remember every time the flock had been attacked by an enemy intent on devouring the sheep. I'm certain that David could tell you a story about each time he had to use his rod and staff to protect the flock. Or maybe he would tell you about the time he used his slingshot to ward off a hungry predator. There were times when it may have been tempting to let the predator have one sheep instead of putting his own life on the line.

In First Samuel 17, David had taken some food down to his brothers as the army of Israel was engaged in a war with the Philistines. When David arrived at the camp of Israel, he could hear the Philistine warrior Goliath, a giant of a man, mocking the Israeli army and defying the God of Israel. When David asked his brothers why they were not engaging the enemy in battle, they rebuked him and told him to go back home and take care of the sheep.

When David saw the fear on the faces of his brethren and heard Goliath defying the God of Israel, he wondered aloud, *"Is there not a **cause**?"* (1 Sam. 17:29). In other words, David was appalled that no one in Israel seemed to trust God enough to accept the challenge of the enemy. David boldly stepped up to the plate and declared that *he* would go out and fight against Goliath. Saul, the king of Israel, tried to discourage David from fighting the enemy. He reminded David that Goliath was an experienced warrior who had been fighting all his life and that David was *just* a shepherd boy with no experience in warfare. David responded by recounting the times when a lion and a bear had attacked the sheep and had taken a lamb out of the flock. David not only delivered the lamb from the beast, but when the animal came after him he grabbed it by the throat and killed it. Remember, a good shepherd never flees in the face of danger. Notice where David's confidence came from:

> *Thy servant slew both the lion and the bear: and this uncircumcised Philistine shall be as one of them, seeing he hath defied the armies of the living God. David said moreover,* ***The Lord*** *that delivered me out of the paw of the lion, and out of the paw of the bear,* ***He will deliver*** *me out of the hand of this Philistine...* (1 Samuel 17:36-37).

David understood that God always *had his back* when he was out in the field with his father's sheep, and he was confident that God would *have his back* if he were to engage Goliath in battle! Through time and experience, David came to understand that God's goodness and mercy were always there to back him up in every situation he encountered with his enemy.

In addition to all the external challenges David had to face in protecting the flock, he also had to feed, comfort, and nurture the sheep. He was responsible for tending to the various cuts and bruises sustained by the sheep every day. Because of the nature of sheep, they could be easily distracted, frightened, and intimidated. However, the shepherd, through his soothing, familiar voice and gentle, tender touch, would constantly reassure the sheep that they had nothing to fear because he was there. With a relationship built over time on nurture and protection, the sheep came to expect that each day would be followed by the next with the same care and protection from their good shepherd! In the same manner, your Good Shepherd is watching and protecting you at all times. You now have two twin companions that follow you every day of your life. They are *goodness* and *mercy*.

Beneficiaries of God

What is the goodness of the Lord? According to *Strong's Exhaustive Concordance of the Bible*, the word *goodness*, in its widest sense, can be translated, "good things, beautiful, best, bountiful, pleasant, pleasure, prosperity, wealth and favor"![1] Take a moment to meditate on the sheer magnitude of God's goodness that is following you. Goodness is also listed as one of the nine fruits of the Spirit in Galatians 5. In Galatians, the word *goodness* suggests the idea of virtue or beneficence. This literally means we are the *beneficiaries* of God! Let's plug in all the various applications of God's goodness upon our lives.

- Surely *good* things will follow me all the days of my life.
- Surely *beautiful* things will follow me all the days of my life.
- Surely the *best* things will follow me all the days of my life.

- Surely *bountifulness* will follow me all the days of my life.
- Surely *prosperity* will follow me all the days of my life.
- Surely *wealth* will follow me all the days of my life.
- Surely *God's favor* will follow me all the days of my life.

You are the beneficiary of all that God has provided through Jesus Christ! Take a few minutes to write or type this list in large, *bold* letters and post it in a spot where you will be reminded of the things that are following you every day you leave your house. Let this *Rhema* (living) word change your daily outlook. Too many of God's people are discouraged, not just because things are going badly now, but because the outlook for tomorrow isn't much better. However, because the Lord is your Shepherd, good things are coming your way! Your expectation and your daily confession should be, "God's blessing and favor are right behind me." Every goal you establish and every enterprise you set your hands to accomplish—*know* that the Good Shepherd is in front of you and His goodness is following you. Every morning when you wake up, look for God's goodness and favor. At the end of a long day, *know* that His goodness is still behind you.

God's mercy, on the other hand, serves another vital purpose in our lives. It can be likened to the oil used by the shepherd to bind up the wounds of the sheep. Mercy has a healing, medicinal effect on the recipient. Again, *Strong's*

Concordance gives us insight into the various shades of meaning for mercy. Mercy can be understood as the issuing forth of God's kindness and favor. It conveys a sense of God's compassion and pity that He bestows upon us.

> *The Lord is merciful and gracious, slow to anger, and plenteous in mercy. He will not always chide: neither will He keep His anger for ever. He hath not dealt with us after our sins; nor rewarded us according to our iniquities. For as the heaven is high above the earth, so great is His* ***mercy*** *toward them that fear Him* (Psalm 103:8-11).

We sometimes don't follow the leading of the Good Shepherd, and like all sheep we tend to go astray. Often our going astray (sins and iniquities) will cause us to be inflicted with bruises and wounds. However, God's mercy is so awesome that it allows Him to be kind toward us and not punish us as our sins might deserve. In fact, God's tender mercies are over *all* His works (see Ps. 145:9). Think of that! God's *mercy* is over *all* His works. Put another way, *God's mercy* ***supersedes*** *His judgment!* Take a moment to consider these important facts about God's mercy.

God's thoughts toward us are *good* thoughts! Contrary to Hollywood's depiction of an angry, vengeful, and austere God who looks for opportunities to exact judgment against humankind, God's thoughts toward us are actually good. Even when God does have to judge us, He tempers His judgment with His mercy!

> *For I know the thoughts that I think toward you, saith the Lord, thoughts of peace, and* ***not*** *of evil, to give you an expected end* (Jeremiah 29:11).

What does this mean for us today? In Exodus 25, Moses was instructed by God to make an ark (wooden box) out of shittim wood. Moses was to overlay the ark with pure gold within and without (see Exod. 25:10-11). God further instructed Moses to put the Testimony, which is the Book of the Law, inside the ark. The ark, containing the Book of the Law or Covenant, was to always stay in the camp of Israel, as it represented the tangible presence of God's throne. By putting the Law inside the ark, God's Word would always be there to judge Israel, especially when they failed to keep the covenant. However, since God's *mercies* are *over* all His works, Moses was instructed to make a *mercy seat* of pure gold that was to be placed *on top* of the ark. On each side of the mercy seat there were two cherubs, also made of pure gold, facing each other. When God wanted to commune (talk) to Israel, He would come and sit between the two cherubim upon the mercy seat! Therefore, when God needed to deal with His children according to His Word, He was always positioned on His *mercy*.

This means you can go forward each day with confidence knowing that the Good Shepherd is leading you in the right path, and even if you stumble and fall, God's mercy is right behind you to pick you up and set you back on the right course.

God proves that His thoughts toward us are good by backing them up with acts of mercy. Mercy is what compels God to be good to man. *Mercy is God's love in action!*

> *For God* ***so*** *loved the world, that* ***He gave*** *His only begotten Son, that whosoever believeth in Him should not perish, but have everlasting life* (John 3:16).

Let me show you a powerful truth in the Word concerning the mercy of God. In Matthew 15, Jesus had arrived at the coastal cities of Tyre and Sidon, just north of the region of Galilee. While there, a Syrophenician woman of Greek ancestry approached Jesus and pleaded with Him to heal her daughter (see Mark 7:26). However, Jesus not only refuses to grant her request, but He actually ignores the woman. Notice the language used by this woman as she petitioned the Lord.

> *...Have mercy on me, O Lord,* ***Thou son of David;*** *my daughter is grievously vexed with a devil* (Matthew 15:22).

The problems the woman faced were both cultural and national in nature. Not unlike today, there existed at that time a great deal of animosity between the Jews and the other nations in the region. So much so that these groups had almost no dealings with each other. The woman had appealed to Jesus using the name of David, thereby invoking the rights of the Jewish covenant. This apparent breach of protocol so infuriated the disciples that they asked Jesus to send the woman away (see Matt. 15:23).

Jesus politely told the woman that under the terms of the Davidic covenant He was only to minister to the Jews. The woman, not to be denied, fell down on her knees worshipping the Lord, and again asked for His help. This time Jesus not only denied the woman's request but appeared to insult her in the process.

> *But He answered and said, It is not meet* [proper, good] *to take the children's bread, and to* ***cast it to dogs*** (Matthew 15:26).

No one ever accused Jesus of being politically correct! However, the Lord was not intentionally insulting the woman but rather getting her to a place where she could receive her miracle. Unfazed by rejection and *unwilling* to take no for an answer, the woman makes her third request. This time, however, she based her appeal solely on *the mercy of God!*

> *And she said, Truth, Lord: yet the dogs eat of the crumbs which fall from their masters' table* (Matthew 15:27).

Jesus was so taken by the great faith and humility of the woman that He immediately granted her request and healed her daughter. Remember, God's *mercy* is over *all* His works. You don't have to be from the right family or the right side of the track to benefit from the mercy of God. It doesn't matter to God what your nationality or ancestry is. You can be a member of the largest church in the world or someone who hasn't been inside a church in years. *God's mercy is over all His works.* When all else fails, cast yourself on the mercy of God. There is something about the cry to

God for mercy that touches His heart like nothing else can. Some of you need to cast aside your own foolish pride and stubborn insistence on doing things your way and humble yourself under the mighty hand of God.

Under His Mercy

Let me take this one step further. Even when we sin, God's mercy allows us to come to Him and receive forgiveness and healing. Many of you have strayed away from your faith. It is easy to get caught up in the trappings of success and riches and forget that God is the source of all blessing. As a nation, we have foolishly decided that God is no longer relevant to our success and achievement. For some time now, we have pursued a course of greed, narcissism, secularism, and hedonism. And in spite of all the things we have acquired and achieved in technology, medicine, and convenience, we are not satisfied. In fact, this may be the angriest, most depressed, suicidal, fearful, discouraged, and restless generation we have had in a long time. The fact is, no person or nation can continue to reject God and stay on top for long. The good news is that when we humble ourselves and fall on the mercy of God, He will deliver us and heal our families and the land. Consider this last but very important point about the mercy of God.

In Revelation 5, there is a book that contains God's judgments that is about to be opened and read. This book, when opened, will set in motion the final course of man's history as we know it. The seven seals will be opened and God will begin to judge all of the nations and peoples of the earth. *However*, even during this time of great tribulation on the earth God will temper His actions with His *mercy!* Just before the book is opened, God reveals that He has golden vials that are filled with incense mingled with the prayers of the saints (see Rev. 5:8). In Revelation 8, we see the purpose of the vials that are full of the prayers of the saints. The seventh seal is opened, which in turn leads to the sounding of the seven trumpets of judgment that are to be unleashed on the earth. *However*, God does something remarkable just before the sounding of the first trumpet.

> *And another angel came and stood at the altar, having a golden censer; and there was given unto him much incense, that he should offer it* ***with the prayers*** *of all saints upon the golden altar which was before the throne. And the smoke of the incense, which came* ***with*** *the prayers of the saints, ascended up before God out of the angel's hand* (Revelation 8:3-4).

This is an awesome picture of the mercy of God in action! First, God has kept in store all of the prayers and intercessions of all the saints throughout time for this exact moment in human history. Then, *before* He pours out judgment and wrath upon earth, He calls for the prayers of the saints that are mingled with incense to be waved in front of Him. This refreshes the heart of God and allows Him to be *merciful* even as His judgments are poured out upon earth! At this very moment as I type these words, I am overwhelmed by the presence of God's mercy in my heart! Always remember that the mercy of God is available to you every day.

Every time you get up and leave your house, the Good Shepherd will not only lead you in the right direction, but He will cover your rearguard with His goodness and mercy! This protection is a part of the birthright you received when you were born again. Take a moment to worship God and thank Him for His goodness and mercy.

Endnote

1. James Strong, *Strong's Exhaustive Concordance of the Bible* (Peabody, MA: Hendrickson Publishers, 2007), s.v. "Goodness."

Chapter 11

Home Sweet Home

"And I will dwell in the house of the Lord for ever."

As I pointed out in the Introduction, Psalm 23 has to do with God's care for His people in our everyday lives. The house of the Lord David refers to in this verse was probably a place right there in the present where he could go and fellowship with God at any time. Notice David did not say he would dwell in *Heaven* forever. David said he would dwell in *the house of the Lord* forever. Let's examine these two different concepts.

Change Starts at Home

There is a literal place called Heaven that is separate from earth. This is where God and the angels reside (see Matt. 5:16; Mark 13:32). Jesus, the Son of God, came *from* Heaven and was made flesh in order to redeem man (see John 1:14; Gal. 4:4-5). Then Jesus *ascended back* into Heaven after His resurrection (see 1 Pet. 3:22). David, on the other hand, was talking about a place he could go to at any time right here on earth.

After the shepherd brought the sheep back to the fold at the end of the day, he would secure the gate and set a watch so that the flock would be safe throughout the night. At this point, the sheep are content, albeit tired, having been fed and protected by their good shepherd. A sense of calm and familiarity envelops the flock. If sheep could talk, I imagine a conversation like this: "We had a good day, didn't we?"

"Yeah, that was some good grass we ate today."

"Sure was. Our shepherd always takes good care of us."

"That was a close call today. Billy almost got captured by that wild dog."

"Good thing our shepherd was right there to protect us."

"Well, it's good to be home."

"Yeah, it's good to be home." (In the background you hear the soft, peaceful bleating of the other sheep.)

It has been said that "home is where the heart is." I would like to modify that statement by saying, "Home is where someone who loves you lives." Thousands of people, if not millions, go to the house where they live every evening, but they have no sense of being *home*.

Kids hang out with their friends as long as they can, often because they have little connectedness with their family. Husbands and wives stay at work or out with friends and co-workers to avoid the tension and strife they feel when they are at home. Some people stop off for drinks at a bar during the so-called "happy hour" just to prepare for the hell they are going to deal with at home. Something is wrong with this picture!

Home should be the place you go to escape the stress and pressure *from* the outside world. It should be filled with people you love and people who love you. A typical day might include sitting in backed-up traffic during the so-called "rush hour," then working long, hard hours on a job you might not particularly enjoy. Some might have to deal with a difficult boss or co-worker. The fact is, you could handle all these external stressors and more if your home was a place of peace, rest, and protection. Most of the problems we see played out in society are a direct reflection of the turmoil that exists within the home. In 30 years of ministry to families and prisoners, I have noted that the majority of the problems stem from domestic issues.

Where do you turn for answers? Who do you go to for solutions? The *experts* seem to be lost themselves. Politicians, business leaders, educators, and even religious leaders grapple with these problems, apparently unable or unwilling to help people find their way back home. In fact, too many of the caregivers have enriched themselves at the expense of the people they should be serving.

> *Ye eat the fat, and ye clothe you with wool, ye kill them that are fed: but ye feed not the flock. The diseased have ye not strengthened, neither have ye healed that which was sick, neither have ye bound up that which was broken, neither have ye brought again that which was driven away, neither have ye sought that which was lost; but with force and with cruelty have ye ruled them* (Ezekiel 34:3-4).

What a scathing indictment from the Lord against the shepherds of our day! What good is a watchdog that cannot bark? How can you guide if you cannot see? What good is a prophet if he refuses to speak? How can you warn of danger if you are asleep at the wheel?

Fortunately, there is a way for us to turn ourselves around and come back home. There is a *biblical, practical,* and *doable* way to:

- Re-establish our own lives
- Re-establish our families and homes
- Re-establish our nation.

Let me caution you now. This is usually when the conehead professors and so-called experts begin to snicker and scoff at what I am going to say to you. However, we are going to let the experts continue to impress and fool themselves while we get to the heart of the matter and effectuate change!

The root of the problem lies within a serious disconnect that too many of us have within ourselves. This disconnect is not between children and parents or husbands and wives. The problems that exist within those relationships are mere symptoms of a larger, deeper concern. To put it bluntly, we have been severed from our source. *Our source is God!*

With each passing generation, humankind seems hell-bent on getting as far away from God as it possibly can. And as long as you remain disconnected from God you will continue to be a part of the problem and not the solution. Some may argue that historically religion has done more harm than good to society. I agree, but I'm not talking about *religion.* I certainly acknowledge that organized religion has done many wonderful things for society. However, I also must acknowledge that it has done irreparable damage to millions and turned multitudes away from God. Churches great and small are filled each Sunday with disconnected people who are looking for a way out of their dilemmas. They come in with a bag full of problems and in need of an encounter with God. They leave with a bag full of problems and a membership application! Too many of you sit in churches, synagogues, and mosques every week listening to wonderful sermons and beautiful music, but you remain disconnected from God. You *need* to come home to *God*. Remember, home is where someone who loves *you* resides.

How do you come home to God? Someone may ask, "Don't I have to die and go to Heaven in order to be at home with God?" No! God is actually near to you right now. In fact, you can be physically in your house, driving in your car, working at your job, flying in an airplane, lying in a hospital bed, or even confined in a prison cell and *still* be at home in God!

> *The Lord is my light and my salvation; whom shall I fear? the Lord is the strength of my life; of whom shall I be afraid? ... One thing have I desired of the Lord, that will I seek after; that I may* ***dwell in the house of the Lord all the days of my life****, to behold the beauty of the Lord, and to* ***enquire in His temple.*** *For in the time of trouble He shall hide me in His pavilion:* ***in the secret of His tabernacle shall He hide me...*** (Psalm 27:1,4-5).

Even in a time of severe trouble and stress we can be at home in God. To be at home with God is to be filled with His conscious presence (His Spirit) in our hearts. Someone might ask, "How do I get God into my heart? Shouldn't I find a church first? Don't I have to get myself together first? Won't I need a preacher to find God?" All these things can be helpful, but they are not necessary for you to come to God. In fact, I want you to brace yourself for the greatest revelation you will ever receive. Are you ready? *Just ask God to come into your home (heart)!* In John's Gospel, the Lord declared that He would receive *all* that came to Him (see John 7:37).

In Luke 11, Jesus said everyone who asks will receive, everyone who seeks will find, and everyone who knocks, the door will be opened to him (see Luke 11:10). Remember, it doesn't matter who you are or what your station in life is. God is not concerned with your natural blood line.

You can't impress God with the things you possess. You certainly can't influence God by how good *or* bad you have been. God loves you unconditionally! It is past time that you were reconnected to your Good Shepherd. He is your source of life and peace. It's time to come home.

Being at home in God is a *spiritual* place, not a *physical* place. When you are reconnected to God, all that He is and has is now in you. Think of it this way–God's peace will automatically be in your home when you get there because it's already in you! When you go to work you're not looking for peace and harmony, you're bringing it *with* you. When you are confronted with a problem or unexpected crisis, you can still dwell in the house of the Lord even while *still* in the midst of the trouble.

> *Now therefore ye are no more strangers and foreigners, but* ***fellowcitizens*** *with the saints, and of the* ***household*** *of God; and are built upon the foundation of the apostles and prophets, Jesus Christ Himself being the chief corner stone ... In whom ye also are builded together for an* ***habitation*** *of God through the Spirit* (Ephesians 2:19-20,22).

When you come home to God, you become a part of His household. God lives at home with His people because that is where *someone who loves Him lives!*

Dual Citizenship

I want to show you several powerful truths that can be gleaned from the Scripture we just read. The apostle

Paul refers to us as fellow citizens of the household of God. What does it mean to be a citizen of a particular state or country?

- Native (born) there or a naturalized person
- Entitled to the rights and privileges of the country
- Entitled to the protection of the government
- Owe allegiance to the government
- Remain a citizen with all rights even when traveling abroad

When a person becomes a Christian, he or she becomes a citizen of God's Kingdom. This means you now have *dual* citizenship. Remember, you are a citizen of the country of your birth. For example, I was born in Baltimore, Maryland. That automatically made me a citizen of the United States. You also are a citizen of your parent's country even if you are born outside of their native land. If my parents had been out of the country when I was born, I would still be a citizen of the United States. When I became a Christian, I automatically became a citizen of Heaven because of my Parent (God). In John 3, Jesus told Nicodemus, a ruler of the Jews, that in order to know God he must be *born again*. Nicodemus had no idea what Jesus was talking about and asked for an explanation. Jesus told Nicodemus that to be born again meant being born of (through) the Spirit of God.

> *Jesus answered, Verily, verily, I say unto thee, Except a man be born of water and of the Spirit, he cannot enter into the kingdom of God* (John 3:5).

Jesus went on to explain that this new birth granted the right of citizenship and therefore entry into Heaven, the Kingdom of God.

By virtue of the new birth, you are now a citizen of Heaven. And even though you were born outside of the country (Heaven), you can still enjoy the rights and privileges of citizenship! Here are a few of them:

- Fellowship with God
- Healing for the spirit, soul, and body
- The indwelling Holy Spirit
- The blessings of God
- The protection of God

These are only a few of the benefits you now have as a child of God.

Let's take this revelation one step further. As a citizen of Heaven living here on earth, I am a representative of the Kingdom of God. Someone who is a citizen of one country and represents that country while living somewhere else is referred to as an *ambassador*. An ambassador is an official representative of his own government while residing in another country.

As a Christian, you have automatically been *appointed* an *ambassador* of the Kingdom of God here on earth!

> *To wit, that God was in Christ, reconciling the world unto Himself, not imputing their trespasses unto them; and hath committed unto us the word of reconciliation. Now then we are* ***ambassadors*** *for Christ, as though God did beseech you by us: we pray you in Christ's stead, be ye reconciled to God* (2 Corinthians 5:19-20).

The ambassador, while in a foreign country, lives within the confines of the *embassy*. The embassy is not just an official residence but it is considered to be an ***actual*** *part of the country the ambassador is from!*

In other words, when the ambassador is in the embassy, it's as if he is *home*. Foreigners are *not* allowed to come in unless they have been invited. In addition, as an ambassador I enjoy the privilege of *diplomatic immunity!* This means I am not subject to the laws and conditions of the foreign country I am residing in. (Pardon me while I praise God for a minute!) Do you understand what this means?

This means that wherever you may physically be, you are *always* at home with your Good Shepherd! It doesn't matter how bad the conditions are getting around you. When you are at home with the Lord there is a sense of peace and quiet assurance. The news may be all bad on the outside, but you know in your heart that the Good Shepherd will make a way for you.

The storms of economic collapse, political ineptitude, natural disasters, never-ending wars, and moral decay are all around us. But you can be at home with the Good Shepherd. Let not your heart be troubled. Find your way back home to God.

> *He that dwelleth in the secret place of the most High shall abide under the shadow of the Almighty. I will say of the Lord, He is my refuge and my fortress: my God; in Him will I trust* (Psalm 91:1-2).

It is time to get reconnected with your Source. Your life is *just starting*. Your dreams may have faded, but they are not dead. Your vision can and will come to pass. It's time to start living and stop sitting around waiting for doomsday. The *Lord* is your Shepherd. He is all that you need.

Pray:

> *My heavenly Father, I acknowledge that You are God and beside You there is no other. I thank You for Your providential care and the daily provisions You give to me. I humble myself under Your mighty and merciful hand. I ask that You forgive me of all my faults, failures, mistakes, and sins. I thank You that through the death, burial, and resurrection of Jesus Christ, my Good Shepherd, I will not only enjoy eternal life with You*

forever, but I will enjoy Your abundant life right here, right now. Fill my heart with Your Spirit and Presence. In the midst of my storms, I will be at home in You. Cause me to fulfill my creative purpose in this life. In Jesus' matchless name I pray, amen.

May the presence and power of the Lord, our Good Shepherd, rest and abide with you always. Be at peace with God and one with another.

About Mitchell H. Warren

Mitchell H. Warren is the founder and pastor of Word and Faith Fellowship, an interdenominational church and ministry located in Baltimore, Maryland. The ministry began in November 1983 as a small inner-city ministry that has since reached thousands with the life-changing Gospel of Jesus Christ. Dr. Warren has produced and trained many ministers who are currently preaching and teaching the Gospel message to this generation.